MW01625455

Five-Spice Beef with
Udon Noodles & Bok Choy (page 22)

INSTANT POT® SOUPS

ALEXIS MERSEL

PHOTOGRAPHY BY

ERIN SCOTT

weldonowen

CONTENTS

Winter Root Vegetable Soup (page 94)

Chicken, Escarole & Parmesan
(page 56)

SOUP'S ON!

Soup is arguably the world's most perfect food. It is nourishing, warming, and filling, and the flavor combinations for this meal in a bowl are countless. I have always loved making soup, but before the Instant Pot® came into my life, I didn't prepare it as often as I would have liked. It was either an hours-long affair—simmering a whole chicken on the stove on a Sunday afternoon—or a last-minute weeknight dinner—throwing whatever leftovers I could find in the fridge into some stock from the freezer. Now I'm cooking soups from scratch in record time (I'm obsessed with the 30-minute Whole Chicken Soup on page 48) and preparing family-friendly meals (mine loves the Chicken Pot Pie Soup on page 61) every night of the week.

From classics like Carrot-Ginger (page 114) and French Onion (page 106) to fresh ideas using modern ingredient combos (try the Turkey Meatball & Farro on page 69), this book is packed with more than 70 soup recipes in every style and flavor and to suit every season. Whether you're a first-time Instant Pot® user or a pressure-cooking pro looking for new ideas, there is something here for you. You can personalize these soups and stews to your own taste by swapping in alternative ingredients. Try spinach for kale, chickpeas for cannellini beans, pepper Jack for Monterey Jack. And don't forget the toppings! A sprinkling of fresh herbs, a drizzle of sour cream, a scattering of crumbled bacon—an inspired garnish can make everyday soup something special.

I've been a champion of my electric pressure cooker for a while, which led me to develop and write the first two titles in this series, *Everyday Instant Pot®* and *Healthy Instant Pot®*. Focusing on just soups and stews has been an exciting and interesting challenge, and I discover new things every day. Before you dive into this collection of fast, flavorful, and fun recipes, take time to understand how the pot works (see the primer on page 8) and learn the secrets to creating soup in it (page 14). Once you master the Instant Pot®, cooking in it will become second nature. Homemade stock (pages 124–126) is ready in a fraction of the time it would take on the stove, and makes all the difference. Experiment with a few recipes from each chapter to start building your repertoire. This book has everything you'll need to become a pro in no time.

Bon appétit!

INSTANT POT® PRIMER

Welcome to a new world of fast, even, flavorful cooking. The Instant Pot® cuts cooking times to a fraction of what's typical, so traditionally long-simmered dishes are ready in record time. Soups come together in minutes, not hours, making a cozy weekend favorite possible any night of the week.

HOW DOES IT WORK?

The tightly sealed pot boils liquid quickly, then traps the steam and generates pressure. With pressure cooking, heat is evenly, deeply, and quickly distributed. The Instant Pot® is available in a selection of models and sizes, each with slightly different cooking features and programs. A general rule of thumb regarding size is if you're primarily cooking for 4 to 6 people, a model with a 6-quart (6-L) capacity should be sufficient. If you're feeding a crowd of 8 or more, a pot with an 8-quart (8-L) capacity is a better choice. The recipes in this book were developed and tested using the Duo Plus 6-Quart Instant Pot®. If you've just purchased an Instant Pot®, read the user manual first to get comfortable with your model's parts, buttons, settings, and indicator lights.

FUNCTIONS & SETTINGS

Each model has slightly different cooking features, with up to eighteen distinct cooking programs to choose from, depending on the model. You can essentially sauté, sear, steam, simmer, slow cook, pressure cook, and braise in this machine. Since not all the models have all the settings, most of the recipes in this book rely on just two functions, Pressure Cook (Manual on some older models), which is a pressure setting, and Sauté, a non-pressure setting. Many recipes call for both functions, either starting with a sauté step followed by pressure cooking, or pressure cooking first and then finishing on the Sauté function. It might seem like a lot of fuss, but once you get the hang of it, it won't feel that way at all. Just think about all the time and effort you will be saving by not having to transfer food from pot to pot or stove to oven and back again!

Most models have several settings specific to a type of food, such as Soup/Broth, Meat/Stew, Bean/Chili, Cake, Egg, Rice, Multigrain, Porridge, and Yogurt. These functions have automatic programs set to the amount of time and pressure level needed for most dishes in the respective category, but you can adjust them as needed. Experiment using these programs to make the recipes you cook often, and soon some of your household's most popular dishes will be set-and-forget meals. Some models have a Sterilize function as well, which is handy for sterilizing bottles and jars easily and efficiently, though only the Max line of pots is safe for pressure canning. The Max also has a Sous Vide function, altitude adjustments, automated steam release, and a touch-screen interface.

Chicken Enchilada Stew (page 53)

Sauté: This function allows you to sear meat, simmer stock, reduce liquid, and more, similar to how you use a sauté pan on the stove. It has three modes: Less is ideal for cooking bacon or other foods that might stick; Normal is best for simmering, thickening, and reducing liquids; and More is handy for browning meat. The timer on this function is automatically set for 30 minutes, but in the rare case when you might need it on for longer than that, just press the Sauté button again after it has shut off and continue cooking. Never put the locking lid on while using this function.

Pressure Cook: There are two levels for pressure cooking, High and Low. Most recipes call for the High setting. The low setting can be used for delicate foods like fish or eggs. Press the Pressure Level key or Adjust key (depending on your model) to adjust pressure levels, and the + and - keys to change the cooking time. (The Lux 6-in-1 V3 model does not have a low-pressure setting.)

Slow Cook: This is a non–pressure cooking program, where the Less, Normal, and High modes correspond to the low, medium, and high settings in some temperature-controlled slow cookers. It works similarly to a traditional slow cooker, cooking food very, very slowly with more liquid than required for pressure cooking. You can use this function for preparing your favorite slow-cooker recipes.

Steam: Always use the steam rack that came with the pot, or a metal or silicone steam basket, when using this program. The pot comes to pressure on full, continuous heat, and the food can scorch if it's not raised off the bottom of the pot.

Keep Warm/Cancel: These buttons, sometimes combined into one, turn off any cooking program, allowing you to switch to another program or to end cooking. The Keep Warm setting holds the food at a safe temperature for up to 10 hours.

Delay Start: This feature allows you to delay the start of cooking, particularly handy if you want to soak dried beans before cooking them.

COOKING UNDER PRESSURE

The pressure release valve (also called steam release valve) has two positions: Venting and Sealing. The pot can come up to pressure only when the lid is locked and the valve is set to Sealing. As a safety precaution, you will not be able to open the lid unless the valve is first set to Venting. There are two main ways to release the pressure when the program ends.

Quick Release: Manually turn the valve to Venting as soon as the cooking program has ended. Take caution when moving the valve: use an oven mitt, wooden spoon, or kitchen tongs instead of bare hands, and do not put your face over or near the valve, as the steam will shoot out quickly.

Natural Release: The pot will lose pressure on its own as it cools. The time needed for a natural pressure release varies depending on the volume of food and liquid in the pot (the greater the amount, the longer it will take), and can be as quick as a few minutes or as long as 30 minutes. Once the program has finished, the pot defaults to the Keep Warm setting and will remain there for up to 10 hours.

You can also perform a combination of the two releases, letting the pressure release naturally for a few minutes and then turning the valve to Venting to quick-release any residual steam. Each recipe in this book indicates the optimal method, whether it be quick release, natural, or a combination of the two. But it helps to understand why you are choosing one over another. Two factors contribute to which method you would choose for steam release:

(1) Whether the dish is hearty and would benefit from sitting longer (such as a soup, stew, or braised meat dish), or if the dish involves delicate foods that require only a few minutes of cooking time (such as pasta or vegetables) and would not benefit from a longer cooking or resting time.

(2) How much liquid is in the pot.

The first factor is often pretty straightforward. The dishes in this book generally feature hearty ingredients and a lot of liquid, two components that call for a natural pressure release or a combination. The second factor is a safety issue. It's important to know that the steam releases from the valve with great intensity. With soups or other dishes containing a lot of liquid, there will be more steam releasing and more potential for hot water splattering over your kitchen or any people nearby. Although it might be hard to wait a little longer to enjoy your meal once it has finished cooking, don't be hasty with releasing the steam manually.

LIQUID LEVELS

Unlike a slow cooker, which allows liquids to evaporate and reduce during cooking, a pressure cooker is completely sealed and therefore loses no steam during cooking. The liquid level is made up of all wet ingredients, including stock, water, wine, canned tomatoes with juice, and the like. The pot cannot come up to pressure unless it has enough liquid, so you'll want to make sure you have the minimum amount required for your model. The amount needed depends on the size of your pot. For a 3-quart (3-L) pot, the amount is 1½ cups (350 ml); for a 6-quart (6-L) pot, it is 2 cups (475 ml); and for an 8-quart (8-L) pot, it is 3 cups (700 ml).

Also, be sure to respect the fill line: to allow room for the steam buildup, the inner pot should never be more than two-thirds full.

PRESSURE COOKING PRACTICALITIES

- To come up to pressure, the pot needs enough steam buildup, which is created from the amount of liquid in the recipe. (Keep in mind that ingredients like vegetables have liquid in them, too.)
- The valve might feel a bit wobbly when switching between Venting and Sealing.
- A little steam coming out of the valve is normal when the pot is coming up to pressure.
- The program timer will not start until the machine has reached pressure.
- For safety reasons, you cannot remove the lid from the pot when it is cooking under pressure. All of the pressure needs to be released first.

Instant Pot Max
www.InstantPot.com
Pressure Cook
Sauté/ Brown
Rice
Steam
Pre-Heat
On
Pressure
Temperature
61
Keep Warm
Venting
Delay
Canning
Yogurt
Cancel
Start

The Instant Pot® is a one-stop shop for building layers of flavor when making soup. Start by cooking base ingredients in oil on the Sauté mode for a few minutes, then add heartier, flavor-rich ingredients and the stock for pressure cooking, and finish with delicate ingredients that require gentle cooking.

SOUP HOW-TOS

Many aspects of cooking soup carry over from one recipe to another. Make the most of your meal—and your Instant Pot®—with a handful of key soup-specific strategies.

THE SECRETS TO PERFECT SOUP

- Many soups start with the same three base ingredients, onions, carrots, and celery, which are sometimes referred to as a *mirepoix* (in French) or *soffritto* (in Italian). This trio, which is typically cooked in oil or butter until softened, is often the first step in building flavors in soups, stews, and stocks. Chop up a good-size batch of each vegetable and store the batches in airtight containers in the fridge for up to 3 days to make quick work of future soup prep.

- Because of their high liquid levels, soups will take longer to come up to pressure than other Instant Pot® meals, so allow a little extra time in your meal prep for that step. But the good news is that it's all hands-off time!

- Dried beans cooked in the Instant Pot® do not require presoaking. They will cook along with the other ingredients. Beans may be presoaked as a matter of preference, though cooking time should adjust accordingly (see page 129).

- If you use homemade stock, which is likely to be less salty than store-bought, be sure to taste and add more salt if needed before serving.

- Add quick-cooking ingredients, such as shrimp, fish, corn, and kale, to the hot liquid after pressure cooking. This will help tender vegetables keep their vibrant color and will prevent delicate seafood from overcooking.

- After browning meat or cooking bacon, adding chopped onion to the pot will make easy work of scraping up the browned bits on the bottom of the pot. Once the onions start to release some liquid, use a wooden spoon to stir them well and dislodge the browned bits. You can also add a few tablespoons of stock or wine to help along this deglazing.

- Cook bacon on the Sauté Less mode: press the Sauté button until the display shows "Less." This will help prevent the bacon from sticking to the bottom of the very hot pot.

- If a recipe begins with cooking bacon, you can omit the bacon and use oil in place of the fat.

- When cooking onions or leeks, use the times provided in the recipes as a guide, as their cooking time will depend on how fresh they are. Softer, older onions and leeks will cook more quickly than fresher, firmer ones.

- Canned tomatoes are great to have on hand for last-minute meals. If a recipe calls for diced tomatoes and you have none on hand, you can also use canned whole tomatoes and break them up with a wooden spoon.

- Grated garlic and ginger are delicate and will likely burn if cooked on the Sauté mode. But it's fine to add either one to a pot of liquid or to a mixture for making meatballs (like the Turkey Meatball & Farro, page 69).

- The topping and garnish suggestions in these recipes aren't just a pretty face! They will enhance the flavor and often the texture of the finished soup, so don't skip them. Many recipes have a list of ideas to choose from, so feel free to personalize toppings to your taste. Try to keep parsley on hand in your fridge at all times, as it is a great way to brighten the flavor of almost any soup.

- Pasta can be cooked in a soup or separately, depending on the recipe and on whether the whole batch of soup will be eaten in a single meal. When pressure cooking, the cooking times are based on the size of the pasta, so it's important to use the shape suggested or something similar. For example, the macaroni in Garlicky Pork, Macaroni & Red Kale (page 38) cooks in just 2 minutes, so if you'd like to swap it for something else, pick a similar-size shape. Always use a quick release when cooking pasta so it doesn't overcook or get mushy. If it is likely you will have leftover soup, cook the pasta separately and divide it among the serving bowls. If the pasta sits in the soup, it will continue to absorb liquid and become too soft.

- An immersion blender, or handheld blender, will be your best friend when making puréed soups. Because it allows you to blend ingredients right in the Instant Pot®, it will save you the trouble of transferring the hot liquid to a blender either after or in the middle of cooking.

- Let soups cool completely before freezing them. Pint (475-ml) and quart (950-ml) deli containers are ideal for portioning and freezing big batches and leftovers.

- Some foods need very little cooking time or no pressure cooking at all. Tender vegetables can be cooked quickly on the Sauté mode at the end of cooking. Delicate fish and shellfish need only brief simmering in a soup or curry. If a dish comes out undercooked to your taste, it is easily remedied. Just re-cover the pot, lock the lid, bring the machine back up to pressure, and cook for a few more minutes. Once the food in the pot is warm, it will take less time to return to pressure, so any additional cooking will be much quicker.

TOOLS OF THE TRADE

A few key tools are essential to preparing a selection of recipes in this book. They include:

Kitchen tongs for browning meat and transferring it from the pot to a plate; quick-releasing the steam valve safely; and holding a paper towel for removing fat from the pot after sautéing meat

Fat separator to degrease soups and sauces

Standard blender or immersion blender for puréeing soups

INSTANT POT® ACE BLENDER

All of the soup purées in this book can also be prepared using the Instant Pot® Ace Blender, which has a built-in heating element and four hot blending programs to cook and purée ingredients in the same vessel. For information, visit www.instantpot.com.

TIPS & TRICKS

Once you're familiar with the basics of your machine, the fun begins. The more you use the Instant Pot®, the more comfortable you'll feel and the more adept you will become at customizing recipes and cooking times to your preference. These key pointers will help you get started.

- Cut ingredients into similarly sized pieces so they cook evenly. This applies to everything from meat and seafood to vegetables. Size and cooking time are also related, as bigger pieces will take longer to cook. Take note of the sizes indicated for ingredients such as pork, beef, carrots, potatoes, and root vegetables, as cooking times are proportionate to the size they have been cut.
- Pat meat dry before cooking in fat for better and more even browning.
- It's often easier and more time efficient to cook chicken pieces whole, then shred or cut them after cooking.
- Use kitchen tongs to grasp paper towels for quickly and easily wiping out unneeded fat from the pot during or after cooking.
- To prevent burning your hands from the hot steam, use kitchen tongs or a wooden spoon to open the steam valve when releasing pressure.
- During steam release, make sure the pot is at a safe distance from any surfaces that could be damaged by excess water, such as wooden cabinets. Always tilt the lid away from you when removing it from the pot so steam doesn't hit your face.
- The inner pot can get quite hot while on the Sauté mode, which means ingredients cut into small pieces can sometimes cook too quickly and start to stick or burn. If this happens, you can use a little stock, wine, or water to help deglaze the pot, stirring to loosen the browned bits from the pot bottom (many recipes include specific instructions for this). Use a wooden spoon and stir continually while cooking to help prevent this from happening.
- Never fill the pot more than two-thirds full, to allow enough room for steam to build, or more than half full when cooking rice or beans, to give them room to expand.
- Adding cornstarch or flour before pressure cooking can result in settling and clumping at the bottom of the pot, which can cause improper heat dispersion and scorching. Use cornstarch or flour to thicken soups and stews after pressure cooking to avoid this situation.
- And finally, one of the most important general rules of cooking is also essential here: taste your food and adjust the seasonings (salt, pepper, herbs, and spices) before you serve it. Flavors develop throughout the cooking process—and especially during a final simmering stage—so fine-tuning the taste just before serving is almost always necessary.

Rainbow Minestrone (page 98)

Posole Rojo with Pork (page 43)

BEEF & PORK

Five-Spice Beef with Udon Noodles & Bok Choy

Economical beef cuts like blade and flat-iron become fork-tender when cooked under pressure. Shichimi togarashi, a Japanese seven-spice seasoning blend, makes a flavorful garnish.

SERVES 4–6

2 small or 1 large shallot, minced (about 3 tablespoons)

2-inch (5-cm) piece fresh ginger, peeled and minced (about 1 tablespoon)

½ teaspoon Chinese five-spice powder

4 cups (950 ml) beef stock (page 125 or store-bought)

2 cups (480 ml) water

2 lb (1 kg) boneless beef blade, flat-iron, or beef chuck steak, cut into slices against the grain ¼ inch (6 mm) thick

Kosher salt

4 heads baby bok choy, trimmed and quartered lengthwise

1 package (about 10 oz/285 g) dried udon noodles

1 teaspoon sugar

FOR SERVING

Minced green onions, shichimi togarashi (optional)

Combine the shallot, ginger, five-spice powder, stock, water, beef, and 2 teaspoons salt in the Instant Pot® and stir to mix.

Lock the lid in place and turn the valve to Sealing. Press the Pressure Cook button and set the cook time for 30 minutes at high pressure.

Let the steam release naturally for 15 minutes, then turn the valve to Venting to quick-release any residual steam. Carefully remove the lid. Using tongs, transfer the beef to a plate. Carefully pour the broth through a fine-mesh sieve set over a heatproof bowl. Return the strained broth to the pot. Press the Cancel button to reset the program.

Press the Sauté button twice to select More mode. Add the bok choy and noodles and cook until just tender, about 5 minutes. (If you don't plan to eat the all of the soup in one sitting, cook the noodles separately according to the package directions and add them in individual portions so they don't get mushy.) Stir in the sugar and taste and adjust the seasoning if needed.

Ladle the soup into bowls and top with green onions. Sprinkle with shichimi togarashi, if desired.

Short Rib Stew

Falling-off-the-bone-tender short ribs cook in the Instant Pot® in a fraction of the time of a traditional stove-top braise. For a thicker consistency, cook the liquid on the Sauté mode for about 10 minutes after you transfer the cooked ribs to a plate.

SERVES 4–6

3 lb (1.4 kg) beef short ribs

Kosher salt and freshly ground black pepper

2–3 tablespoons olive oil

1 yellow onion, chopped

2 ribs celery, sliced

1 carrot, peeled, halved lengthwise, and cut into half-moons ½ inch (12 mm) thick

6 cloves garlic, minced

1 cup (240 ml) dry red wine

2 bay leaves

4½ cups (1.1 L) beef stock (page 125 or store-bought)

1 cup (200 g) dried white beans, picked over and rinsed

1 can (15 oz/425 g) diced tomatoes and their juice

¼ cup (15 g) chopped fresh flat-leaf parsley, plus more for serving

Pat the short ribs dry with paper towels. Season generously with salt and pepper.

Select Sauté on the Instant Pot® twice to select More mode and heat 1 tablespoon of the oil. Working in batches, add the short ribs and brown on both sides, about 8 minutes total. If the meat begins to stick, add another tablespoon oil. As each batch is ready, transfer to a plate.

Add 1 tablespoon of the oil and the onion, celery, and carrot to the pot and cook, stirring occasionally, until softened, about 5 minutes. Add the garlic and cook, stirring, until fragrant, about 1 minute. Add the wine and cook, stirring to dislodge any browned bits from the pan bottom, until absorbed, about 2 minutes. Add the bay leaves, stock, beans, tomatoes, and 1 teaspoon salt and stir to mix. Press the Cancel button to reset the program.

Lock the lid in place and turn the valve to Sealing. Press the Pressure Cook button and set the cook time for 40 minutes at high pressure.

Let the steam release naturally, or for at least 15 minutes before turning the valve to Venting to quick-release any residual steam. Carefully remove the lid and discard the bay leaves. Transfer the ribs to a plate, let sit until cool enough to handle, then remove the meat from the bones. If desired, skim off and discard some of the fat from the surface of the liquid. Return the meat to the pot and stir in the parsley. Taste and adjust the seasoning if needed.

Ladle the stew into bowls and top with parsley and pepper.

Classic Beef Chili

Beef chuck, kidney beans, and a heady mix of spices meld together beautifully when cooked under pressure. Set out bowls of sour cream, shredded Cheddar, and sliced green onions and let guests dress their own bowls on game day.

SERVES 4–6

3 lb (1.4 kg) boneless beef chuck, excess fat trimmed, cut into 1-inch (2.5-cm) cubes

Kosher salt

3 tablespoons canola oil

1 yellow onion, chopped

2 cloves garlic, minced

3 tablespoons ancho chile powder

1 tablespoon paprika

2 teaspoons ground cumin

1 teaspoon dried oregano

2½ cups (600 ml) water

½ cup (115 g) tomato paste

1 cup (200 g) dried red kidney beans, picked over and rinsed

FOR SERVING

Sour cream, grated Cheddar cheese, and/or sliced green onions

Pat the beef dry with paper towels. Season lightly all over with salt.

Select Sauté on the Instant Pot® and heat 2 tablespoons of the oil. Working in batches, add the beef and brown evenly on all sides, about 8 minutes for each batch. As each batch is ready, transfer to a plate.

Add the remaining 1 tablespoon oil and the onion to the pot and cook, stirring occasionally, until softened, about 5 minutes. Add the garlic and cook, stirring, until fragrant, about 1 minute. Stir in the chile powder, paprika, cumin, and oregano, mixing well. Pour in the water, then stir in the tomato paste until blended. Return the beef and any accumulated juices to the pot, add the beans, and stir to coat with the sauce. Press the Cancel button to reset the program.

Lock the lid in place and turn the valve to Sealing. Press the Pressure Cook button and set the cook time for 20 minutes at high pressure.

Let the steam release naturally. Carefully remove the lid and let the chili stand for 5 minutes to allow the flavors to settle.

Ladle the chili into bowls and top each serving with sour cream, cheese, and/or green onions, as desired.

Make easy substitutions to suit your taste. Try ground turkey instead of beef and pepper Jack in place of the Jack-Cheddar combo.

Mac 'n' Cheese Chili

The perfect marriage of two favorite comfort foods, this recipe is all about the cheese. Stir a generous helping into the hot chili and add more as a topping, along with a handful of sliced jalapeños to lighten up the rich ingredients.

SERVES 6

2 tablespoons olive oil

½ yellow onion, diced

2 cloves garlic, minced

1 lb (450 g) lean ground beef

1 tablespoon chili powder

1½ teaspoons ground cumin

1 can (15 oz/425 g) fire-roasted diced tomatoes and their juice

1 cup (170 g) dried pinto beans

4 cups (950 ml) chicken stock (page 124 or store-bought)

Kosher salt and freshly ground black pepper

2 cups (200 g) dried small pasta shells

1 cup (120 g) shredded sharp Cheddar cheese

1 cup (120 g) shredded Monterey Jack cheese

3 green onions, chopped

FOR SERVING (OPTIONAL)
Shredded Cheddar cheese, shredded Monterey Jack cheese, chopped green onions, sliced jalapeño chiles

Select Sauté on the Instant Pot® and heat the oil. Add the onion and cook, stirring occasionally, until softened, about 3 minutes. Add the garlic and cook, stirring occasionally, until fragrant, about 1 minute. Press the Sauté button again to switch to More mode. Add the ground beef and cook, breaking it up with a wooden spoon, until starting to brown, 5–7 minutes. Add the chili powder, cumin, tomatoes, beans, stock, 1 teaspoon salt, and a pinch of black pepper and stir to mix. Press the Cancel button to reset the program.

Lock the lid in place and turn the valve to Sealing. Press the Pressure Cook button and set the cook time for 22 minutes at high pressure.

Let the steam release naturally for 10 minutes, then turn the valve to Venting to quick-release any residual steam. Carefully remove the lid. Press the Cancel button to reset the program.

Add the pasta and stir to mix. Lock the lid in place and turn the valve to Sealing. Press the Pressure Cook button and set the cook time for 4 minutes at high pressure.

Turn the valve to Venting to quick-release the steam. Carefully remove the lid and stir in the Cheddar and Jack cheeses and green onions. Taste and adjust the seasoning if needed.

Ladle the soup into bowls and top with Cheddar and Jack cheeses, green onions, and jalapeños, if using.

Navy Bean, Ham & Bacon

This meaty, chunky soup is just begging for a big piece of cornbread for dunking. To create the creamy texture, you can purée half of the soup with a blender or just mash as many of the beans as you like with a wooden spoon.

SERVES 4–6

4 slices thick-cut bacon (about 4 oz/115 g total), cut into 1-inch (2.5-cm) pieces

1 tablespoon olive oil

1 yellow onion, chopped

3 cloves garlic, minced

2 ribs celery, sliced

4 cups (950 ml) chicken stock (page 124 or store-bought)

1 cup (200 g) dried navy beans, picked over and rinsed

½ lb (225 g) cooked ham steak, ½ inch (12 mm) thick, cut into ½-inch (12-mm) cubes

Kosher salt and freshly ground black pepper

Select Sauté on the Instant Pot® three times to select Less mode and add the bacon. Cook, stirring occasionally, until the bacon is browned and most of the fat is rendered, 5 minutes. Using a slotted spoon, transfer the bacon to a paper towel–lined plate. Grasp a paper towel with tongs and wipe out all but 1 tablespoon of fat from the pot.

Heat the oil in the pot. Add the onion, garlic, and celery and cook, stirring occasionally, until softened, about 5 minutes. Press the Cancel button to reset the program.

Add the stock, beans, 1 teaspoon salt, and ½ teaspoon pepper and stir to combine. Lock the lid in place and turn the valve to Sealing. Press the Pressure Cook button and set the cook time for 25 minutes at high pressure.

Let the steam release naturally, or for at least 15 minutes before turning the valve to Venting to quick-release any residual steam. Carefully remove the lid. Transfer half the soup to a blender and blend until smooth. Return the puréed soup to the pot and stir to mix. (Alternatively, transfer half the soup to a bowl and use an immersion blender to blend the soup in the pot. Return the chunky soup to the pot and stir to mix.) Or for a rustic soup, mash some of the beans in the pot with a wooden spoon. Taste and adjust the seasoning if needed.

Ladle the soup into bowls and top with the bacon and pepper.

Pork & Vegetable Ramen

Customize this homey noodle soup with your choice of toppings. Fresh ramen, which can be found in the refrigerated section of well-stocked grocery stores or Asian markets, will taste best, but dried noodles are a respectable substitute.

SERVES 6

2 lb (1 kg) boneless pork shoulder, cut into 3 equal pieces

Kosher salt

1 tablespoon canola oil

1 yellow onion, chopped

6 cloves garlic, chopped

2-inch (5-cm) piece fresh ginger, peeled and chopped

8 cups (2 L) chicken stock (page 124 or store-bought)

1 leek, white and pale green parts only, halved lengthwise, rinsed well, and sliced

¼ lb (115 g) cremini or white button mushrooms, brushed clean and sliced

1½ lb (680 g) fresh or dried ramen noodles

1 tablespoon soy sauce, plus more if needed

FOR SERVING

Baby bok choy, sliced napa cabbage, sliced fresh shiitake mushrooms, peeled and halved soft-boiled eggs, sliced green onions, sesame seeds, and/or roasted nori seaweed strips, plus toasted sesame and/or chile oil

Pat the pork dry with paper towels. Season generously all over with salt. Select Sauté on the Instant Pot® and heat the oil. Working in batches, add the pork and brown evenly on all sides, about 5 minutes per side. As each batch is done, transfer it to a plate. Grasp a paper towel with tongs and wipe out all but 2 tablespoons of fat from the pot.

Add the onion to the pot and cook, stirring occasionally and scraping up any browned bits, until softened, about 3 minutes. Add the garlic and ginger and cook, stirring, until fragrant, about 1 minute. Add 1 cup (240 ml) of the stock and cook for 1 minute. Press the Cancel button to reset the program.

Add the leek, mushrooms, and remaining 7 cups (1.7 L) stock and stir to mix. Return the pork to the pot. Lock the lid in place and turn the valve to Sealing. Press the Pressure Cook button and set the cook time for 45 minutes at high pressure.

Meanwhile, cook the noodles according to the package directions and set aside.

Let the steam release naturally for 20 minutes, then turn the valve to Venting to quick-release any residual steam. Carefully remove the lid. Transfer the pork to a plate, let cool slightly, then shred into bite-size pieces with two forks. Strain the broth through a fine-mesh sieve set over a heatproof bowl. Discard the solids, reserving the mushroom slices if desired. Skim off the fat from the surface of the broth. Add the soy sauce, then taste and add more soy if needed.

Divide the noodles among 6 bowls and ladle the broth over the noodles. Add the pork and toppings.

Beef Pho

A rich, aromatic broth plays the leading role in this popular Vietnamese street food. Thinly sliced beef cooks in the broth, so it's best to serve the soup piping hot. Set out a big tray of the toppings and allow diners to serve themselves.

SERVES 4

4-inch (10-cm) piece fresh ginger, cut into 4 pieces

1 lb (450 g) shallots, unpeeled

7 whole star anise pods

5 whole cloves

2 cinnamon sticks

8 cups (1.9 L) beef bone broth or beef stock (page 125 or store-bought)

2 carrots, cut crosswise into thirds

Kosher salt

1 package (about 8 oz/225 g) dried flat rice noodles

3–4 tablespoons fish sauce

2–3 teaspoons sugar

½ lb (225 g) beef sirloin, frozen for 1 hour

FOR SERVING

Fresh cilantro leaves, fresh basil leaves (preferably Thai), mung bean sprouts, sliced jalapeño, lime wedges, Sriracha sauce, hoisin sauce

Select Sauté on the Instant Pot®. Add the ginger and shallots to the dry pot and cook, turning occasionally with tongs, until slightly colored, about 5 minutes. Add the star anise, cloves, and cinnamon sticks and cook, stirring occasionally, until fragrant, about 2 minutes. Press the Cancel button to reset the program.

Add the broth, carrots, and 1 teaspoon salt to the pot and stir to mix. Lock the lid in place and turn the valve to Sealing. Press the Pressure Cook button and set the cook time for 30 minutes at high pressure.

Cook the noodles according to the package directions and set aside.

Let the steam release naturally, or for at least 15 minutes before turning the valve to Venting to quick-release any residual steam. Carefully remove the lid. Strain the broth through a colander or fine-mesh sieve set over a heatproof bowl. Return the broth to the pot. Press the Cancel button to reset the program.

Press the Sauté button twice to select the More mode. Bring the broth to a boil. Add 3 tablespoons of the fish sauce and 2 teaspoons of the sugar and stir well. Taste and adjust the seasoning as needed.

While the broth is heating, cut the partially frozen beef on the diagonal against the grain into paper-thin slices. Arrange the herb and vegetable toppings in individual piles on a large platter.

Divide the noodles evenly among 4 bowls. Top with the beef, dividing it evenly. Ladle the hot broth on top of the beef and noodles. Serve with the platter of toppings and hoisin and Sriracha alongside for diners to add as desired.

Fresh cilantro and Thai basil leaves, sliced jalapeño, and a squeeze of lime help keep the flavors bright.

Bacon, Sausage & White Bean Cassoulet

The name of this French country stew comes from *cassole*, the traditional vessel in which it is cooked. Instead of hours, this version cooks in just 40 minutes and relies on thick-cut bacon and smoked sausage for its rich, succulent flavor. Accompany the cassoulet with a green salad to balance the richness.

SERVES 4–6

4 slices thick-cut smoked bacon (about 4 oz/115 g total), chopped

1 lb (450 g) fully cooked smoked sausages, cut into slices ½ inch (12 mm) thick

1 yellow onion, chopped

2 carrots, chopped

4 cloves garlic, minced

1 cup (240 ml) dry white wine

2½ cups (600 ml) chicken stock (page 124 or store-bought)

2 tablespoons firmly packed dark brown sugar

1 tablespoon Dijon mustard

¼ teaspoon ground coriander

1 bay leaf

Kosher salt and freshly ground black pepper

1 cup (200 g) dried white beans, such as cannellini or Great Northern, picked over and rinsed

FOR SERVING

Chopped fresh flat-leaf parsley leaves, crusty bread

Select Sauté on the Instant Pot® three times to select Less mode and add the bacon. Cook, stirring occasionally, until browned and most of the fat is rendered, about 5 minutes. Using a slotted spoon, transfer the bacon to a paper towel–lined plate. Add the sausages and cook, stirring occasionally, until starting to brown, about 5 minutes. Using the slotted spoon, transfer the sausage slices to a separate plate. Grasp a paper towel with tongs and wipe out all but 2 tablespoons of fat from the pot.

Add the onion and carrots to the pot and cook, stirring occasionally, until they start to brown, 5–7 minutes. (If you see lots of dark brown bits threatening to burn on the pot bottom, add 1 tablespoon of the wine to the pot now and stir to dislodge them.) Add the garlic and cook, stirring, until fragrant, about 1 minute. Add the wine and bring to a simmer, stirring occasionally with a wooden spoon to scrape up any browned bits. Cook until the wine is reduced by almost half, about 2 minutes. Add the stock, brown sugar, mustard, coriander, bay leaf, and a few grindings of pepper, stir well, and bring to a simmer. Press the Cancel button to reset the program.

Return the bacon and sausages to the pot. Add the beans, and stir to mix. Lock the lid in place and turn the valve to Sealing. Press the Pressure Cook button. Set the cook time for 40 minutes at high pressure.

Let the steam release naturally. Carefully remove the lid and remove and discard the bay leaf. Taste and adjust the seasoning with salt and pepper.

Ladle the stew into bowls and top with parsley. Serve with bread.

Tuscan Tomato, White Bean & Bacon

You can make this hearty, comforting Italian-style soup year-round with just a handful of pantry staples and some bacon from the fridge. Adding spinach at the end of cooking delivers a slightly sweet taste and a rich color, but the soup will still be delicious without it.

SERVES 6

3 slices thick-cut bacon (about 3 oz/90 g total), cut into 1-inch (2.5-cm) pieces

1 yellow onion, chopped

3 cloves garlic, minced

4 cups (950 ml) chicken stock (page 124 or store-bought)

1 cup (200 g) dried white beans, such as cannellini or Great Northern, picked over and rinsed

1 can (14½ oz/410 g) diced tomatoes and their juice

Kosher salt and freshly ground black pepper

2 cups (90 g) firmly packed baby spinach (optional)

½ cup (30 g) chopped fresh basil

FOR SERVING

Freshly grated Parmesan cheese

Select Sauté on the Instant Pot® three times to select Less mode and add the bacon. Cook, stirring occasionally, until browned and most of the fat is rendered, about 5 minutes. Using a slotted spoon, transfer the bacon to a paper towel–lined plate. Grasp a paper towel with tongs and wipe out all but 2 tablespoons of fat from the pot.

Add the onion to the pot and cook, stirring occasionally and scraping up any browned bits, until softened, about 5 minutes. Add the garlic and cook, stirring, until fragrant, 1 minute. Add the stock, beans, tomatoes, half of the bacon, 1 teaspoon salt, and ¼ teaspoon pepper and stir to combine. Press the Cancel button to reset the program.

Lock the lid in place and turn the valve to Sealing. Press the Pressure Cook button and set the cook time for 40 minutes at high pressure.

Let the steam release naturally for 15 minutes, then turn the valve to Venting to quick-release any residual steam. Carefully remove the lid. Immediately add the spinach, if using, and basil. The spinach will wilt in the hot liquid in about 3 minutes. Taste and adjust the seasoning if needed.

Ladle the soup into bowls and top with the remaining bacon and with cheese.

Portuguese Kale, Sausage & Potato Soup

This crowd-worthy and comforting winter bowl is a modern take on caldo verde, the classic Portuguese soup featuring a robust combo of meat, potatoes, and leafy greens. Thanks to pressure cooking, the cooked sausage slices become meltingly tender, attaining a delicate, meatball-like texture.

SERVES 6

1 tablespoon olive oil

1 yellow onion, chopped

4 cloves garlic, minced

1½ lb (680 g) Yukon Gold potatoes, quartered

1 can (15 oz/425 g) diced tomatoes and their juice

1 cup (170 g) dried red kidney beans

¾ lb (340 g) Portuguese chouriço or linguiça or Spanish chorizo sausages, sliced ½ inch (12 mm) thick

6 cups (1.4 L) chicken stock (page 124 or store-bought)

1 bay leaf

½ teaspoon smoked paprika

Kosher salt and freshly ground black pepper

1 bunch Tuscan kale, stemmed and coarsely chopped or torn into large pieces

FOR SERVING
Crusty bread

Select Sauté on the Instant Pot® and heat the oil. Add the onion and garlic and cook, stirring occasionally, until the onion starts to soften and the garlic is fragrant, about 3 minutes. Add the potatoes, tomatoes, beans, sausage, stock, bay leaf, paprika, 1 teaspoon salt, and ¼ teaspoon pepper and stir to mix. Press the Cancel button to reset the program.

Lock the lid in place and turn the valve to Sealing. Press the Pressure Cook button and set the cook time for 20 minutes at high pressure.

Let the steam release naturally, or for at least 15 minutes before turning the valve to Venting to quick-release any residual steam. Carefully remove the lid and discard the bay leaf. Immediately add the kale and stir to mix. The kale will wilt in the hot liquid in about 3 minutes. Taste and adjust the seasoning if needed.

Ladle the soup into bowls and serve with bread alongside.

French Beef Stew

If you prefer a thicker consistency for this Gallic-inspired stew, dissolve 1 tablespoon cornstarch in 1 tablespoon cold water and stir the slurry into the broth after releasing the pressure, then cook on the Sauté mode for 8–10 minutes.

SERVES 4

3 lb (1.4 kg) beef chuck, excess fat trimmed, cut into 2-inch (5-cm) cubes

Kosher salt and freshly ground black pepper

2 slices thick-cut bacon (about 2 oz/60 g total), diced

1 tablespoon canola oil

1 cup (240 ml) beef stock (page 125 or store-bought)

1 yellow onion, chopped

2 ribs celery, sliced

3 cloves garlic, smashed

1 tablespoon tomato paste

1 cup (240 ml) red wine

1 lb (450 g) Yukon Gold potatoes, cut into 2-inch (5-cm) pieces

3 carrots, peeled and cut into 1½-inch (4-cm) chunks

2 fresh thyme sprigs

1 bay leaf

1 tablespoon Worcestershire sauce

FOR SERVING

Chopped fresh flat-leaf parsley leaves, crusty French bread

Pat the meat dry with paper towels. Season with 2 teaspoons salt and 1 teaspoon pepper.

Select Sauté on the Instant Pot® and add the bacon. Cook, stirring occasionally, until browned and most of the fat is rendered, about 5 minutes. Using a slotted spoon, transfer the bacon to a paper towel–lined plate.

Add the oil to the pot. Working in batches, add the beef and brown evenly on all sides, about 8 minutes for each batch. As each batch is ready, transfer to a plate. Add 1 tablespoon of the stock and stir with a wooden spoon to scrape up any browned bits. Add the onion and celery and cook, stirring occasionally, until beginning to soften, about 3 minutes. Add the garlic and tomato paste, stir to mix, and cook, stirring, for about 1 minute. Add the remaining stock and the wine and cook for 1 minute. Press the Cancel button to reset the program.

Return the beef to the pot, add the potatoes, carrots, thyme, bay leaf, and Worcestershire sauce, and stir to mix. Lock the lid in place and turn the valve to Sealing. Press the Pressure Cook button and set the cook time for 25 minutes at high pressure.

Let the steam release naturally. Carefully remove the lid. Press the Cancel button to reset the program.

Press the Sauté button and bring the stew to a simmer. Cook until thickened, 3–5 minutes; the timing depends on the desired thickness. Remove and discard the thyme sprigs and bay leaf. Taste and adjust the seasoning if needed.

Ladle the stew into bowls and top with parsley. Serve with bread.

Beef Barley

A rich, tomatoey beef broth studded with nutrient-packed barley is the perfect winter warmer. Don't leave out the chopped herbs at the end, as they brighten the flavor of this hearty soup.

SERVES 6

2 lb (1 kg) boneless beef chuck or stew meat, excess fat trimmed, cut into 1-inch (2.5-cm) cubes

Kosher salt and freshly ground black pepper

1 tablespoon olive oil

1 yellow onion, chopped

5 cups (1.2 L) beef or chicken stock (pages 124–125 or store-bought)

3 carrots, peeled and cut into slices ½ inch (12 mm) thick

2 ribs celery, sliced

½ lb (225 g) cremini mushrooms, brushed clean and sliced

2 cloves garlic, minced

½ cup (125 g) tomato purée

1 cup (200 g) pearl barley

1 bay leaf

1 tablespoon chopped fresh dill

FOR SERVING

Chopped fresh dill, chopped fresh flat-leaf parsley

Pat the beef dry with paper towels. Season with 1½ teaspoons salt and ½ teaspoon pepper.

Select Sauté twice on the Instant Pot® to select More mode and heat the oil. Working in batches, add the beef and brown evenly on all sides, about 8 minutes total. As each batch is ready, transfer to a plate.

Add the onion and 1 tablespoon of the stock to the pot, stirring with a wooden spoon to scrape up any browned bits. Cook, stirring occasionally, until the onion starts to soften, about 3 minutes. Add the carrots, celery, and mushrooms and cook, stirring occasionally, until softened, about 4 minutes. Add the garlic and cook, stirring, until fragrant, about 1 minute. Add the tomato purée and remaining stock and stir to combine. Press the Cancel button to reset the program.

Return the beef and its juices to the pot, add the barley, bay leaf, ½ teaspoon salt, and ½ teaspoon pepper and stir to mix. Lock the lid in place and turn the valve to Sealing. Press the Pressure Cook button and set the cook time for 30 minutes at high pressure.

Let the steam release naturally for 10 minutes, then turn the valve to Venting to quick-release any residual steam. Carefully remove the lid, discard the bay leaf, and stir in the dill. Taste and adjust the seasoning if needed.

Ladle the soup into bowls and top with dill and parsley.

Garlicky Pork, Macaroni & Red Kale

The pasta and pork in this flavorful soup cook together in just 2 minutes! That's because pork tenderloin is naturally tender, so it cooks under pressure in much less time than many other cuts. Any type of kale—red, curly, Tuscan, Redbor, Siberian—can be used, or you can substitute Swiss chard or spinach.

SERVES 4

1 lb (450 g) pork tenderloin, cut in half crosswise

Kosher salt and freshly ground black pepper

1 tablespoon olive oil

½ yellow onion, chopped

5 cloves garlic, minced

5 cups (1.2 L) chicken stock (page 124 or store-bought)

1 bunch red or other kale, stemmed and coarsely chopped or torn into large pieces

1 can (15 oz/425 g) diced tomatoes and their juice

1 cup (100 g) dried macaroni

Pat the pork dry with paper towels. Season generously with salt.

Select Sauté on the Instant Pot® and heat the oil. Add the pork and brown evenly on both sides, about 3 minutes per side. Using tongs, transfer to a plate.

Add the onion, garlic, and 1 tablespoon stock to the pot, stirring to scrape up any browned bits, and cook until the onion is softened, about 2 minutes. Add the kale, ½ teaspoon salt, and a pinch of pepper and cook, stirring occasionally, until the kale is starting to wilt, about 2 minutes. Add the remaining stock, tomatoes, and macaroni and stir to mix. Press the Cancel button to reset the program.

Lock the lid in place and turn the valve to Sealing. Press the Pressure Cook button and set the cook time for 2 minutes at high pressure.

Let the steam release naturally for 10 minutes, then turn the valve to Venting to quick-release any residual steam. Carefully remove the lid. Transfer the pork to a plate and let cool for 5 minutes. (After the 5 minutes, the pork should read 145–155°F/63°–68°C on an instant-read thermometer.) Cut the pork against the grain into slices ¼ inch (6 mm) thick and return the pork to the pot. Taste and adjust the seasoning as needed.

Ladle the soup into bowls and serve.

Red kale is similar to curly kale, except for the ruddy red hue in its stems and often also its leaves.

Italian Wedding Soup

The origin of the name for this southern Italian soup comes from the "marriage" of flavors between the meat and greens. Traditionally simmered on the stove top for hours, this version comes together quickly, and the meatballs cook to tender perfection under pressure.

SERVES 6

FOR THE MEATBALLS

1 lb (450 g) ground pork

2 cloves garlic, minced or grated

¼ cup (15 g) panko bread crumbs

2 tablespoons freshly grated Parmesan cheese, plus more for serving

1 egg, lightly beaten

1 tablespoon tomato paste

1 teaspoon dried oregano

Kosher salt and freshly ground black pepper

6 cups (1.4 L) chicken stock (page 124 or store-bought)

3 large carrots, peeled and chopped

1 rib celery, sliced

1 lb (450 g) kale, escarole, or other sturdy leafy green, stemmed and chopped

1 cup (½ lb/225 g) acini di pepe pasta ("peppercorns" shape)

To make the meatballs, in a bowl, combine the pork, garlic, bread crumbs, cheese, egg, tomato paste, oregano, 1 teaspoon salt, and ¼ teaspoon pepper. Using your hands or a wooden spoon, mix gently just until all the ingredients are evenly distributed. Be careful not to overmix, or the meatballs will be tough. To shape each meatball, scoop up a heaping teaspoon of the turkey mixture and, using lightly dampened hands, roll it into a ball between your palms. As the meatballs are shaped, set them aside on a large plate. You should have about 30 meatballs.

Combine the stock, carrots, celery, meatballs, 1 teaspoon salt, and ¼ teaspoon pepper in the Instant Pot®. Lock the lid in place and turn the valve to Sealing. Press the Pressure Cook button and set the cook time for 15 minutes at high pressure.

Let the steam release naturally for 10 minutes, then turn the valve to Venting to quick-release any residual steam. Carefully remove the lid. Press the Cancel button to reset the program.

Press the Sauté button and bring the broth to a simmer. Add the kale and pasta and cook until the pasta starts to soften and kale is wilted, about 4 minutes. (The pasta will continue to soften as it sits in the hot broth.) Taste and adjust the seasoning if needed.

Ladle the soup into bowl and top with Parmesan cheese and pepper.

Korean Beef Stew

Common Korean ingredients of kimchi, ginger, red onion, and gochujang (a spicy, sweet, hot chile paste) come together in this robust stew bursting with flavor. For a thicker stew, after transferring the ribs to a plate, bring the liquid to a simmer on the Sauté mode and cook for 8–10 minutes.

SERVES 4–6

4 lb (1.8 kg) beef short ribs

Kosher salt and freshly ground black pepper

2 tablespoons canola oil

1 red onion, finely chopped

1 carrot, peeled and chopped

2 cups (480 ml) chicken or beef stock (pages 124–125 or store-bought)

1 tablespoon minced garlic

2-inch (5-cm) piece fresh ginger, peeled and minced

½ cup (120 ml) low-sodium soy sauce

½ cup (60 g) kimchi

¼ cup (75 g) gochujang

¼ cup (60 g) firmly packed dark brown sugar

FOR SERVING

Sliced green onions, toasted sesame seeds

Pat the ribs dry with paper towels. Season with salt and pepper.

Select Sauté on the Instant Pot® twice to select More mode and heat the oil. Working in batches, add the short ribs and brown the meat evenly, about 8 minutes total for each batch. As each batch is done, transfer it to a plate. Grasp a paper towel with tongs and wipe out all but 1 tablespoon of fat from the pot.

Add the red onion, carrot, and 1–2 tablespoons of the stock to the pot and cook, stirring occasionally and scraping up any browned bits, until the onion is softened, about 5 minutes. Add the garlic and ginger and cook, stirring, until fragrant, about 1 minute. Add the remaining stock, the soy sauce, kimchi, gochujang, sugar, ½ teaspoon salt, and ¼ teaspoon pepper and stir to mix. Press the Cancel button to reset the program.

Return the short ribs to the pot. Lock the lid in place and turn the valve to Sealing. Press the Pressure Cook button and set the cook time for 40 minutes at high pressure.

Let the steam release naturally, or for at least 15 minutes before turning the valve to Venting to quick-release any residual steam. Carefully remove the lid. Transfer the ribs to a plate, set aside until cool enough to handle, then remove the meat from the bones. If desired, skim off and discard some of the fat from the surface of the liquid. Return the meat to the pot, then taste and adjust the seasoning if needed.

Ladle the stew into bowls. Top with green onions and sesame seeds.

Posole Rojo with Pork

The toppings and tortillas are as essential to this centuries-old Mexican soup as the pork, hominy, and spices. Choose a selection of pretty bowls, fill them with the suggested toppings, and set them out on a big platter or tray.

SERVES 6

2 lb (1 kg) boneless thick-cut pork chops (about 4), excess fat trimmed

Kosher salt and freshly ground black pepper

2 tablespoons canola or avocado oil

1 large yellow onion, chopped

8 cloves garlic, minced

2 tablespoons tomato paste

2 tablespoons chili powder

1½ teaspoons dried oregano, preferably Mexican

½ teaspoon dried thyme

4 cups (950 ml) chicken stock (page 124 or store-bought)

1 cup (240 ml) water

1 can (25 oz/710 g) hominy, rinsed and drained

FOR SERVING

Shredded green cabbage, thinly sliced radishes and jalapeño chiles, diced onions (red, yellow, or white), sour cream, fresh cilantro leaves, charred corn tortillas, lime wedges

Pat the pork dry with paper towels. Season the pork generously with salt and pepper.

Select Sauté on the Instant Pot® and heat 1 tablespoon of the oil. Working in batches, add the pork and brown evenly on both sides, about 3 minutes per side. As each batch is ready, transfer to a plate.

Add the remaining 1 tablespoon oil and the onion to the pot and cook, stirring occasionally with a wooden spoon and scraping up any browned bits, until softened, about 3 minutes. Add the garlic and cook, stirring, until fragrant, about 1 minute. Add the tomato paste, chili powder, oregano, thyme, and 2 tablespoons of the stock and cook, stirring occasionally, for 1 minute. Press the Cancel button to reset the program.

Add the remaining stock, the water, and the hominy and stir to mix. Return the pork and any accumulated juices to the pot. Lock the lid in place and turn the valve to Sealing. Press the Pressure Cook button and set the cook time for 30 minutes at high pressure.

Let the steam release naturally for 20 minutes, then turn the valve to Venting to quick-release any residual steam. Carefully remove the lid. Using tongs, transfer the pork to a plate. Let the pork sit until cool enough to handle. Then, using two forks, shred it into bite-size pieces. Return the pork to the pot and stir in 1 teaspoon salt. Taste and adjust the seasoning with salt and pepper as needed.

Ladle the soup into bowls and top with cabbage, radishes, onion, sour cream, and/or cilantro, Serve with tortillas and lime wedges alongside.

Irish Stew

Nothing is more Irish than a dark stout, which lends a unique creaminess and richness to this no-fuss stew. Don't skip the browning step, as it adds a lot of flavor and mellows the gamy taste of the lamb.

SERVES 4–6

2 lb (1 kg) boneless lamb leg, cut into 1½–2-inch (4–5-cm) cubes

Kosher salt and freshly ground black pepper

2 tablespoons unsalted butter

1 yellow onion, chopped

2 cups (480 ml) beef stock (page 125 or store-bought)

1 cup (240 ml) stout or brown ale

4 Yukon Gold potatoes, cut into 2-inch (5-cm) chunks

3 carrots, peeled and cut into 1½-inch (4-cm) pieces

FOR SERVING

Chopped fresh flat-leaf parsley, crusty bread

Pat the lamb dry with paper towels. Season with 1½ teaspoons salt and ½ teaspoon pepper.

Select Sauté on the Instant Pot® twice to select More mode and melt the butter. Working in batches, add the lamb and brown evenly on all sides, about 8 minutes per batch. As each batch is done, transfer to a plate. Grasp a paper towel with tongs and wipe out all but 1 tablespoon of fat from the pot.

Add the onion and 1–2 tablespoons of the stock to the pot and cook, stirring occasionally and scraping up any browned bits, until the onion starts to soften, about 3 minutes. Add the remaining stock and the stout and stir to mix. Press the Cancel button to reset the program.

Return the lamb to the pot, add the potatoes, carrots, and 1 teaspoon salt, and stir to combine. Lock the lid in place and turn the valve to Sealing. Press the Pressure Cook button and set the cook time for 30 minutes at high pressure.

Let the steam release naturally, or for at least 15 minutes before turning the valve to Venting to quick-release any residual steam. Carefully remove the lid. If desired, skim off and discard some of the fat from the surface of the liquid Taste and adjust the seasoning if needed.

Ladle the stew into bowls and top with parsley. Serve with bread alongside.

Red Bean Chili with Sausage

Andouille, a spicy smoked pork sausage, is the best choice for this Cajun-inspired meal, but kielbasa or other smoked sausage would also work well. To mellow the spiciness, add a spoonful of steamed rice to every bowl before adding the chili.

SERVES 6

¾ lb (340 g) andouille sausages

1 tablespoon olive oil

1 lb (450 g) ground beef

Kosher salt and freshly ground black pepper

1 yellow onion, chopped

1 green bell pepper, seeded and diced

1 rib celery, diced

4 cloves garlic, minced

2 tablespoons chili powder

1 tablespoon ground cumin

1 teaspoon smoked paprika

1 cup (200 g) dried red kidney beans, picked over and rinsed

1 can (10 oz/285 g) Mexican-style diced tomatoes and their juice

1 can (14½ oz/410 g) crushed tomatoes and their juice

2 cups (480 ml) water

4 green onions, thinly sliced

Cut the sausages in half lengthwise, then cut crosswise into half-moons about ½ inch (12 mm) thick.

Select Sauté on the Instant Pot® and heat the oil. Add the sausage and cook, stirring occasionally, until browned, about 4 minutes. Using a slotted spoon, transfer the sausage to a plate. Add the beef to the pot, season with salt and pepper, and cook, stirring to breaking up the meat with a wooden spoon, until browned, about 4 minutes. Using the slotted spoon, transfer the beef to the plate with the sausage.

Add the onion to the pot and cook, stirring occasionally, until beginning to soften, about 2 minutes. Add the bell pepper, celery, and garlic and cook, continuing to stir, until the vegetables are softened, about 3 minutes. Stir in the chili powder, cumin, paprika, and 1 teaspoon salt and stir to mix. Add the beans to the pot along with the cooked sausage and beef, the diced and crushed tomatoes, and the water and stir to mix. Press the Cancel button to reset the program.

Lock the lid in place and turn the valve to Sealing. Press the Bean/ Chili button and set the cook time for 30 minutes at high pressure.

Turn the valve to Venting to quick-release the steam. Carefully remove the lid. Stir in the green onions and season with salt and pepper.

Ladle the chili into bowls and serve.

Turkey Meatball & Farro (page 69)

CHICKEN

Whole Chicken Soup

A from-scratch chicken soup that would typically cook for at least a couple of hours on the stove top comes together in far less time in the Instant Pot®. Make sure your chicken is small enough to fit into the pot; a bird weighing no more than 4½ pounds (2 kg) is ideal.

SERVES 6–8

FOR THE BOUQUET GARNI

4 cloves garlic

2 bay leaves

Handful of black peppercorns

1 yellow onion, chopped

1 whole chicken, 3–4½ lb (1.4–2 kg)

2 carrots, peeled and sliced

2 ribs celery, sliced

Stems from 1 bunch fresh flat-leaf parsley, tied together with kitchen twine, leaves reserved for serving

Kosher salt and freshly ground black pepper

FOR SERVING (OPTIONAL)

Cooked pasta or steamed rice (page 128), and chopped fresh flat-leaf parsley leaves and/or dill sprigs

To prepare the bouquet garni, put the garlic, bay leaves, and peppercorns onto the center of a piece of cheesecloth about 8 inches (20 cm) long. Roll up the cloth lengthwise around the aromatics and tie each end securely with kitchen twine.

Spread the onion in a single layer on the bottom of the Instant Pot®. Arrange the chicken on top, then tuck the carrot and celery pieces alongside the chicken, followed by the bouquet garni and parsley stems. Fill the pot with water to just below the max fill line.

Lock the lid in place and turn the valve to Sealing. Press the Pressure Cook button and set the cook time for 7 minutes per pound (450 g) of chicken at high pressure. (For example, a 4½-lb/2-kg chicken would cook for 32 minutes.)

Let the steam release naturally. Carefully remove the lid and discard the bouquet garni and parsley stems. Carefully transfer the chicken to a cutting board and let sit until cool enough to handle. Using two forks or your hands, shred the chicken into bite-size pieces, discarding the skin and bones. Return the chicken to the pot, add 2 teaspoons salt, and stir to mix. Taste and adjust the seasoning with salt and pepper, if needed. Stir in cooked noodles or rice, if using.

Ladle the soup into bowls and top with parsley and/or dill, if using.

A bouquet garni of bay leaves, peppercorns, and garlic infuses the broth with a subtle depth of flavor.

Chicken Wild Rice

This creamy, nourishing soup is a staple in Minnesota, where wild rice is the official state grain. Forget to thaw the chicken? You can use frozen thighs without adjusting the cooking time. Just keep in mind that the soup will take longer to come up to pressure.

SERVES 6

2 tablespoons unsalted butter

1 yellow onion, diced

2 carrots, peeled and diced

3 ribs celery, diced

½ lb (225 g) cremini mushrooms, brushed clean and sliced

6 cups (1.4 L) chicken stock (page 124 or store-bought)

1 cup (155 g) wild rice, rinsed

1 lb (450 g) boneless, skinless chicken thighs

2 bay leaves

Kosher salt and freshly ground black pepper

¼ cup (60 ml) heavy cream

½ teaspoon chopped fresh thyme leaves

Select Sauté on the Instant Pot® and melt the butter. Add the onion, carrots, and celery and cook, stirring occasionally, until softened, about 5 minutes. Add the mushrooms and cook, stirring occasionally, until softened, about 2 minutes. Add the stock, wild rice, chicken, bay leaves, 1½ teaspoons salt, and 1 teaspoon pepper and stir to mix. Press the Cancel button to reset the program.

Lock the lid in place and turn the valve to Sealing. Press the Pressure Cook button and set the cook time for 25 minutes at high pressure.

Let the pressure release naturally for 20 minutes, then turn the valve to Venting to quick-release any residual steam. Carefully remove the lid and discard the bay leaves. Using two forks, shred the chicken into bite-size pieces. Add the cream and thyme and stir to mix. Taste and adjust the seasoning as needed.

Ladle the soup into bowls and top with pepper.

Chicken & Lentil

High in protein and fiber and low in calories, lentils are a versatile superfood. Any type of lentil that holds its shape—green, black, or brown—can be used in this soup. Avoid red and yellow lentils, which tend to fall apart when cooked under pressure. For a vegetarian version, leave out the chicken.

SERVES 4–6

1 tablespoon olive oil

1 yellow onion, chopped

3 carrots, peeled and chopped

3 ribs celery, sliced

Kosher salt and freshly ground black pepper

3 cloves garlic, minced

½ teaspoon dried thyme

1 can (28 oz/800 g) whole tomatoes and their juice

4 cups (950 ml) water

1½ lb (680 g) boneless, skinless chicken thighs

1 cup (200 g) green, black, or brown lentils, picked over and rinsed

1 bay leaf

1 tablespoon red wine vinegar (optional)

FOR SERVING

Crusty bread

Select Sauté on the Instant Pot® and heat the oil. Add the onion, carrots, celery, 2 teaspoons salt, and ½ teaspoon pepper and cook, stirring occasionally, until softened, about 5 minutes. Add the garlic and thyme and cook, stirring, until fragrant, about 1 minute. Add the tomatoes and cook, breaking them up with a wooden spoon and stirring, until well mixed, about 2 minutes. Add the water, chicken, lentils, and bay leaf and stir to mix. Press the Cancel button to reset the program.

Lock the lid in place and turn the valve to Sealing. Press the Pressure Cook button and set the cook time for 12 minutes at high pressure.

Let the steam release naturally for 15 minutes, then turn the valve to Venting to quick-release any residual steam. Carefully remove the lid and discard the bay leaf. Stir in the vinegar, if using. Using two forks, shred the chicken into bite-size pieces. Taste and adjust the seasoning if needed.

Ladle the soup into bowls and serve with bread alongside.

Chicken Enchilada Stew

You can feed a crowd on a weeknight with this easy-to-assemble soup. Load it up with the toppings suggested here—kids will love to choose their own—or add other favorites, such as sour cream, diced jalapeños, and salsa. To keep the culinary theme going, serve *dulce de leche* ice cream for dessert.

SERVES 6–8

1 yellow onion, chopped

2 cans (15 oz/425 g each) diced fire-roasted tomatoes and their juice

2 cans (4 oz/115 g each) diced green chiles and their juice

1 cup (200 g) dried black beans, picked over and rinsed

4 cups (950 ml) chicken stock (page 124 or store-bought)

2 tablespoons chili powder

2 teaspoons ground cumin

Kosher salt

2½ lb (1.1 kg) boneless, skinless chicken thighs

Grated zest and juice of 1 lime

FOR SERVING

Shredded Cheddar and/or Monterey Jack cheese, chopped fresh cilantro, diced jalapeño chile, sour cream, tortilla chips, lime wedges

Combine the onion, tomatoes, chiles, beans, stock, chili powder, cumin, and 1½ teaspoons salt in the Instant Pot® and stir to mix. Nestle the chicken pieces into the stock mixture.

Lock the lid in place and turn the valve to Sealing. Press the Pressure Cook button and set the cook time for 20 minutes at high pressure.

Let the steam release naturally for 10 minutes, then turn the valve to Venting to quick-release any residual steam. Using two forks, shred the chicken into bite-size pieces. Add the lime zest and half of the lime juice. Taste and adjust the seasoning with more lime juice and salt if needed.

Ladle the stew into bowls and layer with toppings as desired. Serve with lime wedges alongside.

Chicken Mulligatawny

Originally from southern India, this richly seasoned soup is packed with spices, ginger, and garlic, all of which carry important health benefits, from boosting the immune system and aiding bone health to facilitating digestion. If you prefer to cook the rice directly in the soup, increase the cooking time to 15 minutes.

SERVES 4–6

1½ teaspoons ground coriander

1 teaspoon ground cumin

¼ teaspoon cayenne pepper

¼ teaspoon ground turmeric

1 teaspoon hot curry powder

Kosher salt

1½ lb (680 g) boneless, skinless chicken thighs

1 tablespoon grapeseed or olive oil

1 yellow onion, chopped

3 cloves garlic, minced

2-inch (5-cm) piece fresh ginger, peeled and minced

6 cups (1.4 L) chicken stock (page 124 or store-bought)

Juice of ½–1 lemon

FOR SERVING

Steamed basmati rice (page 128), plain yogurt (optional)

In a bowl, stir together the coriander, cumin, cayenne, turmeric, curry powder, and 1 teaspoon salt. Add the chicken and toss to coat evenly.

Select Sauté on the Instant Pot® and heat the oil. Working in batches, add the chicken and brown evenly on both sides, about 3 minutes per side. As each batch is ready, transfer to a plate. Add the onion, stirring occasionally and scraping up any browned bits, until the onion starts to soften, about 3 minutes. Add the garlic and ginger and cook, stirring, until fragrant, about 1 minute. Press the Cancel button to reset the program.

Return the chicken to the pot and add the stock and ½ teaspoon salt. Lock the lid in place and turn the valve to Sealing. Press the Pressure Cook button and set the cook time for 12 minutes at high pressure.

Let the steam release naturally for 10 minutes, then turn the valve to Venting to quick-release any residual steam. Carefully remove the lid. Add half the lemon juice, taste, and add the remaining lemon juice if desired. Taste and adjust the seasoning if needed.

Ladle the soup over rice in bowls and serve the yogurt alongside, if using.

Khao Soi

This spicy Thai coconut curry soup is seriously addictive. To take it over the top, fry thinly sliced shallots in oil on the stove top until browned and crisp, then add them to the finished soup. Look for fresh Chinese egg noodles in the refrigerated section of Asian markets and well-stocked grocery stores.

SERVES 4

¼ cup (60 g) red curry paste

2 teaspoons Madras curry powder

1 stalk lemongrass, tough outer leaves and root end removed

2 cans (13½ fl oz/400 ml each) full-fat coconut milk

2 cups (480 ml) chicken stock (page 124 or store-bought)

2 lb (1 kg) boneless, skinless chicken thighs

3 fresh or frozen Thai lime leaves

Kosher salt

1 lb (450 g) fresh Chinese egg noodles

2–3 tablespoons fish sauce

1–2 tablespoons light brown sugar

FOR SERVING

Fresh cilantro leaves, thinly sliced raw and/or fried shallots (see note), chile oil, lime wedges

In a small bowl, stir together the curry paste and curry powder. To bruise the lemongrass, using the flat side of a chef's knife, push down firmly on the stalk until it splits open. Cut the stalk into 3-inch (7.5-inch) lengths.

Add the curry paste mixture, coconut milk, and stock to the Instant Pot® and whisk well to combine. Add the chicken, lemongrass, lime leaves, and ½ teaspoon salt. Lock the lid in place and turn the valve to Sealing. Press the Pressure Cook button and set the cook time for 12 minutes at high pressure.

Meanwhile, cook the noodles according to the package directions and set aside.

When the soup has finished cooking, let the steam release naturally for 10 minutes, then turn the valve to Venting to quick-release any residual steam. Carefully remove the lid and discard the lemongrass and lime leaves. Using two forks, shred the chicken into bite-size pieces. Add 2 tablespoons of the fish sauce and 1 tablespoon of the sugar and stir to mix. Taste and adjust the seasoning with more fish sauce and sugar if needed.

Divide the noodles evenly among four bowls and ladle the soup over the noodles. Arrange the cilantro, shallots, chile oil, and lemon wedges on a platter and serve alongside for diners to add as desired.

Chicken, Escarole & Parmesan

Switch up your everyday chicken soup with ingredients an Italian nonna would use. Chopped escarole—its mild bitterness brightened by the addition of lemon juice—boosts both the flavor and the texture, while an abundance of grated Parmesan cheese on top melts into the soup, creating a creamy, salty finish.

SERVES 6

1 tablespoon olive oil

1 yellow onion, chopped

4 cloves garlic, minced

6 cups (1.4 L) chicken stock (page 124 or store-bought)

1½ lb (680 g) boneless, skinless chicken thighs

1 large piece Parmesan cheese rind (cheese grated and reserved for serving)

Kosher salt and freshly ground black pepper

1 head escarole (about ½ lb/225 g), chopped

1–2 tablespoons fresh lemon juice

FOR SERVING

Freshly grated Parmesan cheese

Select Sauté on the Instant Pot® and heat the oil. Add the onion and cook, stirring occasionally, until softened, about 4 minutes. Add the garlic and cook, stirring, until fragrant, about 1 minute. Add the stock, chicken, cheese rind, 1½ teaspoons salt, and ½ teaspoon pepper and stir to mix. Press the Cancel button to reset the program.

Lock the lid in place and turn the valve to Sealing. Press the Pressure Cook button and set the cook time for 12 minutes at high pressure.

Let the steam release naturally for 15 minutes, then turn the valve to Venting to quick-release any residual steam. Carefully remove the lid and remove and discard the cheese rind. Immediately add the escarole and 1 tablespoon of the lemon juice and stir to mix. The escarole will wilt in the hot liquid in about 2 minutes. Using two forks, shred the chicken into bite-size pieces. Taste and adjust the seasoning with salt and pepper and with more lemon juice as needed.

Ladle into bowls and top with cheese and pepper.

Grate fresh Parmesan for serving before you start to cook, slipping the cheese rind into the pot to both flavor and thicken the soup.

Gingery Chicken & Zoodle

This healthy, dump-and-stir dish can be prepared and cooked in minutes, making it a go-to weeknight family supper. Cut the zucchini noodles with a spiralizer, or look for them precut and packaged in your grocery store produce section.

SERVES 6

1 yellow onion, chopped

2 carrots, peeled and sliced ½ inch (12 mm) thick

3 ribs celery, sliced ½ inch (12 mm) thick

6 cups (1.4 L) chicken stock (page 124 or store-bought)

1 bay leaf

1 tablespoon cider vinegar

2-inch (5-cm) piece fresh ginger, peeled and grated

Stems from 1 bunch fresh flat-leaf parsley, tied together with kitchen twine, leaves reserved for garnish

1½ teaspoons chopped fresh thyme leaves, or ¾ teaspoon dried thyme

Kosher salt and freshly ground black pepper

1 lb (450 g) boneless, skinless chicken breasts

2 zucchini, spiralized or cut into ribbons with a vegetable peeler, or 1 package (10 oz/285 g) zucchini noodles ("zoodles")

Combine the onion, carrots, celery, stock, bay leaf, vinegar, ginger, parsley stems, thyme, and 1½ teaspoons salt in the Instant Pot® and stir to mix. Nestle the chicken pieces into the stock mixture.

Lock the lid in place and turn the valve to Sealing. Press the Pressure Cook button and set the cook time for 6 minutes at high pressure.

Let the steam release naturally for 5 minutes, then turn the valve to Venting to quick-release the steam. Carefully remove the lid and discard the bay leaf and parsley stems. Transfer the chicken to a plate. Immediately add the zucchini noodles to the pot and heat until warmed through, about 3 minutes. While the noodles are heating, using two forks, shred the chicken into bite-size pieces. Return the chicken to the pot and stir to combine. Taste and adjust the seasoning if needed.

Ladle the soup into bowls and top with parsley leaves and pepper.

Creamy Chicken & Dumplings

Fluffy buttermilk-chive dumplings are the perfect addition to this creamy chicken stew. If you like, steam the dumplings on the stove top over medium-low heat while the stew is pressure cooking so they'll both be ready at the same time.

SERVES 4–6

2 tablespoons unsalted butter

2 leeks, white and pale green parts only, halved lengthwise, rinsed well, and sliced

2 carrots, peeled, halved lengthwise, and cut into half-moons ¼ inch (6 mm) thick

3 ribs celery, sliced

6 cups (1.4 L) chicken stock (page 124 or store-bought)

2 lb (1 kg) boneless, skinless chicken breasts

1 bay leaf

Kosher salt and freshly ground black pepper

2–4 tablespoons heavy cream

FOR THE DUMPLINGS

1¼ cups (155 g) all-purpose flour

1 teaspoon baking soda

½ teaspoon salt

1 tablespoon chopped fresh chives, plus more for serving

Pinch of cayenne pepper

3 tablespoons cold unsalted butter, cut into small cubes

½ cup (120 ml) buttermilk, plus more if needed

Select Sauté on the Instant Pot® and melt the butter. Add the leeks, carrots, and celery and cook, stirring occasionally, until starting to soften, about 5 minutes. Add the stock and stir to combine. Press the Cancel button to reset the program.

Add the chicken, bay leaf, 1½ teaspoons salt, and ¼ teaspoon pepper. Lock the lid in place and turn the valve to Sealing. Press the Pressure Cook button and set the cook time for 6 minutes at high pressure.

Meanwhile, prepare the dumplings. In a bowl, sift together the flour, baking soda, and salt. Stir in the chives and cayenne. With a pastry blender or a fork, cut in the butter until the mixture resembles coarse cornmeal. Add the buttermilk and stir to mix. Using your hands, shape the dough into a soft ball, adding more buttermilk, 1 teaspoon at a time, if needed for the dough to hold together. It should be slightly sticky but workable. To shape each dumpling, pinch off a generous teaspoon-size piece of dough and roll it between your palms to form a ball. As the dumplings are shaped, set them aside on a large plate.

When the soup has finished cooking, let the steam release naturally for 5 minutes, then turn the valve to Venting to quick-release any residual steam. Carefully remove the lid. Using tongs, transfer the chicken to a plate. Using two forks, shred the chicken into bite-size pieces. Press the Cancel button to reset the program.

Press the Sauté button, add the dumplings to the soup, and cook until a toothpick inserted into the center of a dumpling comes out clean, about 12 minutes. Discard the bay leaf. Stir in 2 tablespoons of the cream, adding more if desired. Taste and adjust the seasoning. Ladle the soup and dumplings into bowls. Top with chives and black pepper.

This homey chicken soup, studded with all the essential ingredients of a classic pot pie, is a family favorite.

Chicken Pot Pie Soup

As its name implies, this is the soup version—minus the crust—of a popular comfort food, and it's laced with all the traditional ingredients of its baked counterpart. The buttermilk biscuits served alongside are equally delicious for breakfast with butter and jam.

SERVES 4–6

1 tablespoon unsalted butter

½ yellow onion, diced

1 lb (450 g) Yukon Gold potatoes, cut into 1-inch (2.5-cm) cubes

2 carrots, peeled, halved lengthwise, and sliced

4 cups (950 ml) chicken stock (page 124 or store-bought)

1½ lb (680 g) boneless, skinless chicken breasts

1 teaspoon dried thyme

Kosher salt and freshly ground black pepper

2 tablespoons cornstarch mixed with 2 tablespoons cold water

1 cup (240 ml) whole milk

1 cup (170 g) fresh or frozen corn kernels

1 cup (140 g) fresh or frozen peas

2 tablespoons heavy cream (optional)

FOR SERVING

Buttermilk biscuits (page 130), optional

Select Sauté on the Instant Pot® and melt the butter. Add the onion and cook, stirring occasionally, until it starts to soften, about 3 minutes. Add the potatoes and carrots and cook, stirring, until well combined, about 2 minutes. Add the stock, chicken, thyme, 1½ teaspoons salt, and ¼ teaspoon pepper and stir to mix. Press the Cancel button to reset the program.

Lock the lid in place and turn the valve to Sealing. Press the Pressure Cook button and set the cook time for 6 minutes at high pressure.

Let the steam release naturally for 5 minutes, then turn the valve to Venting to quick-release any residual steam. Carefully remove the lid. Using tongs, transfer the chicken to a plate and shred with two forks or your hands. Press the Cancel button to reset the program.

Press the Sauté button twice to select More mode. Give the cornstarch mixture a quick stir to recombine, then add to the pot along with the milk and cook until the mixture is bubbling and starts to thicken, 4–5 minutes. Add the corn and peas and cook until starting to soften, about 2 minutes for fresh and 3 minutes for frozen. Return the chicken to the pot. Stir in the cream, if using. Taste and adjust the seasoning if needed.

Ladle the soup into bowls and serve with biscuits (if using) alongside.

Tom Kha Gai

Lemongrass, Thai lime leaves, and Thai chiles are essential to creating the authentic flavor of this effortless soup, so seek them out in an Asian market or a well-stocked supermarket. Peppery, woodsy galangal is a rhizome in the ginger family, but if you can't find it, fresh ginger can be substituted with good results.

SERVES 6

2 stalks lemongrass, tough outer leaves and root end removed

1 lb (450 g) boneless, skinless chicken thighs

2-inch (5-cm) piece fresh galangal or ginger, peeled and thickly sliced

1 yellow onion, sliced

2–4 red Thai chiles, bruised

½ lb (225 g) white button mushrooms, brushed clean and quartered

8 fresh or frozen Thai lime leaves

2 cans (13½ fl oz/400 ml each) full-fat coconut milk

1 cup (240 ml) chicken stock (page 124 or store-bought)

3 tablespoons fish sauce

1 tablespoon coconut or granulated sugar

Juice of 1 lime

FOR SERVING

Fresh cilantro leaves or sprigs, lime wedges

To bruise the lemongrass, using the flat side of a chef's knife, push down firmly on each stalk until it splits open. Cut the stalks into 3-inch (7.5-cm) lengths.

Combine the lemongrass, chicken, galangal, onion, chiles (the number depending on the amount of heat desired), mushrooms, lime leaves, coconut milk, stock, and fish sauce in the Instant Pot®. Lock the lid in place and turn the valve to Sealing. Press the Soup button and set the cook time for 12 minutes at high pressure.

Let the steam release naturally for 15 minutes, then turn the valve to Venting to quick-release any residual steam. Carefully remove the lid and remove and discard the lime leaves, lemongrass, and galangal. Using two forks, shred the chicken into bite-size pieces. Add the sugar and lime juice and stir to combine.

Ladle into bowls and top with cilantro. Serve the lime wedges alongside.

Tortilla Soup

It's surprising how much flavor results from the marriage of a few simple ingredients. Ancho chiles are almost black, but once they are soaked, they turn a deep mahogany and infuse the soup with richness and mellow heat. Mexican oregano has a subtle hint of lime, which enhances the essence of the chiles.

SERVES 6

In a small heatproof bowl, combine the chiles with boiling water to cover and let soak for 10 minutes. Drain and discard the liquid.

In a blender or food processor, combine the rehydrated chiles, tomatoes, onion, garlic, and 1 cup (240 ml) of the stock and process until smooth.

Select Sauté on the Instant Pot® and heat the oil. Working in batches, add the chicken and brown evenly on both sides, about 3 minutes per side. As each batch is ready, transfer to a plate. Press the Cancel button to reset the program.

Add the chile purée, cumin, oregano, 1 teaspoon salt, and ½ teaspoon pepper to the pot and stir to mix. Return the chicken to the pot and add the remaining 5 cups (1.2 L) stock and the bay leaves. Lock the lid in place and turn the valve to Sealing. Press the Pressure Cook button and set the cook time for 20 minutes at high pressure.

Let the steam release naturally for at least 15 minutes, then turn the valve to Venting to quick-release any residual steam. Carefully remove the lid and discard the bay leaves. Using two forks, shred the chicken into bite-size pieces. Taste and adjust the seasoning if needed.

Ladle the soup into bowls and top with avocado, cheese, tortilla chips, cilantro, and a drizzle of sour cream.

3 dried ancho chiles, stemmed, seeded, and torn into pieces

Boiling water, to cover

1 can (14½ oz/410 g) crushed tomatoes and their juice

1 yellow onion, coarsely chopped

3 cloves garlic, coarsely chopped

6 cups (1.4 L) chicken stock (page 124 or store-bought)

2 tablespoons olive oil

2 lb (1 kg) boneless, skinless chicken thighs

1 teaspoon ground cumin

1 teaspoon dried oregano, preferably Mexican

Kosher salt and freshly ground black pepper

3 bay leaves

FOR SERVING

Avocado slices, crumbled Cotija cheese, crushed tortilla chips, chopped fresh cilantro leaves, sour cream

Hearty Chicken & Vegetable

This nourishing one-pot meal is sure to become a staple in your weekday soup repertoire. You can skip the corn and zucchini for an even quicker dish, or use kale, Swiss chard, spinach, or another hearty green in their place.

SERVES 6

1 yellow onion, diced

2 carrots, peeled, halved lengthwise, and cut into half-moons ¼ inch (6 mm) thick

3 ribs celery, sliced

2 cloves garlic, minced

1 lb (450 g) butternut or other winter squash, peeled, seeded, and cut into 2-inch (5-cm) cubes

1 lb (450 g) Yukon Gold potatoes, cut into 2-inch (5-cm) cubes

1½ lb (680 g) boneless, skinless chicken thighs

6 cups (1.4 L) chicken stock (page 124 or store-bought)

2 tablespoons tomato paste

½ teaspoon dried thyme

Kosher salt and freshly ground black pepper

1 zucchini, cut into small cubes

1 cup (170 g) fresh or frozen corn kernels

¼ teaspoon red pepper flakes (optional)

Combine the onion, carrots, celery, garlic, squash, potatoes, chicken, stock, tomato paste, thyme, 1½ teaspoons salt, and ½ teaspoon pepper in the Instant Pot® and stir to mix. Lock the lid in place and turn the valve to Sealing. Press the Pressure Cook button and set the cook time for 12 minutes at high pressure.

Let the steam release naturally for 15 minutes, then turn the valve to Venting to quick-release any residual steam. Carefully remove the lid. Press the Cancel button to reset the program.

Press the Sauté button. Add the zucchini and corn to the pot, stir to combine, and cook until the zucchini is tender and the corn is heated through, about 3 minutes for fresh and 5 minutes for frozen corn. Stir in the red pepper flakes, if using. Using two forks, shred the chicken into bite-size pieces. Taste and adjust the seasoning if needed.

Ladle into bowls and top with additional red pepper flakes, if desired.

Generous cubes of butternut squash achieve an appealing tenderness in just over 10 minutes of cooking time in this vegetable-laden soup.

Posole Verde with Chicken

While the red-based cousin (page 43) of this traditional Mexican dish derives its rich color from tomatoes, this green version gets its iconic hue from chopped tomatillos. After removing the papery husks from the tomatillos, be sure to rinse off their sticky residue—a natural defense against insects.

SERVES 6

2 lb (1 kg) boneless, skinless chicken thighs

Kosher salt and freshly ground black pepper

2 tablespoons olive oil

1 yellow onion, chopped

4 cloves garlic, thinly sliced

1 jalapeño chile, seeded and finely chopped

1 teaspoon dried oregano, preferably Mexican

1 teaspoon ground cumin

1 can (25 oz/710 g) hominy, rinsed and drained

6 tomatillos, husks removed, rinsed, and roughly chopped

Juice of 1 lime

FOR SERVING

Fresh cilantro leaves, avocado slices, lime wedges

Pat the chicken dry with paper towels. Season generously with salt and pepper.

Select Sauté on the Instant Pot® and heat the oil. Working In batches, add the chicken and brown evenly on both sides, about 3 minutes per side. As each batch is ready, transfer to a plate.

Add the onion to the pot and cook, stirring occasionally, until softened and translucent, about 5 minutes. Add the garlic, chile, oregano, cumin, 1 teaspoon salt, and ½ teaspoon pepper and cook, stirring, until fragrant, about 1 minute. Add the hominy and tomatillos and stir to combine. Return the chicken to the pot. Press the Cancel button to reset the program.

Lock the lid in place and turn the valve to Sealing. Press the Soup button and set the cook time for 20 minutes at high pressure.

Turn the valve to Venting to quick-release the steam. Carefully remove the lid. Using two forks, shred the chicken into bite-size pieces. Add the lime juice and stir to mix. Season with salt and pepper.

Ladle the posole into bowls and top with cilantro and avocado. Serve with lime wedges alongside.

Chicken & White Bean Chili

Mix up a big batch of this light and healthy chili and freeze it in small containers so it's easy to thaw and reheat for lunch. But don't forget the toppings! They add great flavor and texture to the chili and are easy to pack separately if you are tucking everything into a lunch box for reheating at work.

SERVES 6

1 tablespoon olive oil

1 yellow onion, chopped

4 cloves garlic, minced

1 tablespoon chili powder

2 teaspoons ground cumin

Kosher salt and freshly ground black pepper

5 cups (1.2 L) chicken stock (page 124 or store-bought)

1 can (4 oz/115 g) diced green chiles and their juice

1 cup (200 g) dried Great Northern beans, picked over and rinsed

1½ lb (680 g) boneless, skinless chicken thighs

2 bay leaves

1 cup (170 g) fresh or frozen corn kernels

FOR SERVING

Sliced or diced avocado, sliced jalapeño chiles, chopped fresh cilantro leaves, tortilla chips

Select Sauté on the Instant Pot® and heat the oil. Add the onion and cook, stirring occasionally, until softened, about 5 minutes. Add the garlic and cook, stirring, until fragrant, about 1 minute. Add the chili powder, cumin, 1 teaspoon salt, and ¼ teaspoon pepper and stir to mix. Press the Cancel button to reset the program.

Add the stock, canned chiles, beans, chicken, and bay leaves to the pot. Lock the lid in place and turn the valve to Sealing. Press the Pressure Cook button and set the cook time for 30 minutes at high pressure.

Let the steam release naturally for at least 15 minutes, then turn the valve to Venting to quick-release any residual steam. Carefully remove the lid and discard the bay leaves. Immediately add the corn and cook until heated through, about 3 minutes for fresh and 5 minutes for frozen corn. Taste and adjust the seasoning as needed.

Transfer half the soup to a blender and blend until smooth. Return the puréed soup to the pot and stir to mix. (Alternatively, transfer half the soup to a bowl and use an immersion blender to blend the soup in the pot. Return the chunky soup to the pot and stir to mix.)

Ladle the soup into bowls and top with avocado, jalapeño, and cilantro. Serve with tortilla chips alongside.

Farro is an ancient Italian wheat variety that provides nutrients and fiber, as well as a pleasing chewy texture, to this wholesome soup.

Turkey Meatball & Farro

A cozy cauldron of meatballs is the perfect comfort food. Farro pairs deliciously with the meatballs, adding heft and a mild earthy flavor. Ground dark-meat chicken can be substituted for the turkey.

SERVES 6

FOR THE MEATBALLS

1 lb (450 g) ground turkey

2 cloves garlic, minced or grated

¼ cup (15 g) panko bread crumbs

2 tablespoons freshly grated Parmesan cheese

1 egg, lightly beaten

1 tablespoon tomato paste

1 teaspoon dried oregano

Kosher salt and freshly ground black pepper

2 tablespoons olive oil

1 yellow onion, chopped

2 cloves garlic, minced

2 tablespoons tomato paste

1 cup (200 g) pearled farro

6 cups (1.4 L) chicken stock (page 124 or store-bought)

1 large bunch Swiss chard, stemmed and chopped

FOR SERVING

Freshly grated Parmesan cheese

To make the meatballs, in a bowl, combine the turkey, garlic, panko, cheese, egg, tomato paste, oregano, 1 teaspoon salt, and ¼ teaspoon pepper. Using your hands or a wooden spoon, mix gently just until all the ingredients are evenly distributed. Be careful not to overmix, or the meatballs will be tough. To shape each meatball, scoop up a heaping teaspoon of the turkey mixture and, using lightly dampened hands, roll it into a ball between your palms. As the meatballs are shaped, set them aside on a large plate. You should have about 30 meatballs.

Select Sauté on the Instant Pot® and heat the oil. Add the onion and cook, stirring occasionally, until softened, about 5 minutes. Add the garlic and cook, stirring, until fragrant, about 1 minute. Add the tomato paste, 1 teaspoon salt, and ¼ teaspoon pepper and cook, stirring, for about 1 minute to blend well. Press the Cancel button to reset the program.

Add the farro, stock, and meatballs to the pot and stir gently to mix. Lock the lid in place and turn the valve to Sealing. Press the Pressure Cook button and set the cook time for 15 minutes at high pressure.

Let the steam release naturally for 10 minutes before turning the valve to Venting to quick-release any residual steam. Carefully remove the lid. Immediately add the chard and stir to mix. The chard will wilt in the hot liquid in about 3 minutes. Taste and adjust the seasoning as needed.

Ladle the soup into bowls and sprinkle with cheese.

Coconut Fish Curry
(page 80)

SEAFOOD

Shrimp Gumbo

A roux is a mixture of equal parts flour and fat cooked together and used to thicken stews and sauces. To achieve the traditional flavor and texture of a gumbo, don't skip this step. Offer hot sauce to add at the table.

SERVES 6

1 tablespoon olive oil

1 lb (450 g) andouille sausages, cut into slices ½ inch (12 mm) thick

FOR THE ROUX

5 tablespoons canola oil

5 tablespoons all-purpose flour

1 yellow onion, chopped

1 red bell pepper, seeded and chopped

1 green bell pepper, seeded and chopped

3 cloves garlic, minced

5 cups (1.2 L) chicken stock (page 124 or store-bought)

1 can (15 oz/425 g) diced tomatoes and their juice

2 bay leaves

1 lb (450 g) okra, stemmed and cut into 1-inch (2.5-cm) pieces

1 cup (155 g) wild rice, rinsed

2 tablespoons Cajun Spice Rub (page 130)

Kosher salt and freshly ground black pepper

1 lb (450 g) shrimp, fresh or frozen, peeled and deveined

Select Sauté on the Instant Pot® and heat the olive oil. Add the sausages and cook, stirring occasionally, until browned, about 4 minutes. Using a slotted spoon, transfer the sausage slices to a plate. Grasp a paper towel with tongs and wipe out the pot.

To make the roux, heat the canola oil in the pot. Add the flour and cook, stirring constantly with a whisk or silicone spatula, until the mixture forms a dark brown paste, 15–20 minutes. (The roux can also be made in a saucepan over medium-high heat on the stove top and then transferred to the Instant Pot®.) Add the onion and bell peppers and cook, stirring often, until softened, about 4 minutes. Add the garlic and cook, stirring, until fragrant, about 1 minute. Gradually add the stock, stirring constantly with the spatula or a wooden spoon to prevent lumps from forming and to scrape up any browned bits. Press the Cancel button to reset the program.

Add the reserved sausages, the tomatoes, bay leaves, okra, rice, spice rub, 1 teaspoon salt, and ¼ teaspoon pepper and stir to mix. Lock the lid in place and turn the valve to Sealing. Press the Pressure Cook button and set the cook time for 20 minutes at high pressure.

Let the steam release naturally for 20 minutes, then turn the valve to Venting to quick-release any residual steam. Carefully remove the lid. Discard the bay leaves. Press the Cancel button to reset the program.

Press the Sauté button, add the shrimp, and cook until pink and opaque, 2–3 minutes for fresh or about 4 minutes for frozen. Taste and adjust the seasoning if needed.

Ladle the gumbo into bowls and serve.

Gumbo is a classic Louisiana recipe and testimony to the region's multicultural heritage.

Crab & Corn Chowder

When corn is in season, definitely opt for fresh corn on the cob to make this creamy seafood chowder. But if you're craving this soup during the winter months, substitute frozen corn kernels and skip the corncob step.

SERVES 4–6

4 slices thick-cut bacon (about 4 oz/115 g total), cut into 1-inch (2.5-cm) pieces

1 yellow onion, chopped

½ lb (225 g) Yukon Gold or russet potatoes, peeled and cut into 1-inch (2.5-cm) cubes

Kernels from 4 large ears corn, corncobs reserved (4 cups/680 g)

4 cups (950 ml) chicken, vegetable, or fish stock (pages 124–126 or store-bought)

1 bay leaf

2 tablespoons chopped fresh thyme, or 2 teaspoons dried thyme

Kosher salt and freshly ground black pepper

1½ cups (350 ml) whole milk

Pinch of red pepper flakes (optional)

½ lb (225 g) fresh lump crabmeat, picked over for shell fragments

FOR SERVING

Chopped fresh flat-leaf parsley or chives

Select Sauté on the Instant Pot® three times to select Less mode and and add the bacon. Cook, stirring occasionally, until the bacon is browned and most of the fat is rendered, about 5 minutes. Using a slotted spoon, transfer the bacon to a paper towel–lined plate. Grasp a paper towel with tongs and wipe out all but 1 tablespoon of fat from the pot. Add the onion and cook, stirring occasionally and scraping up any browned bits, until softened, about 5 minutes. Add the potatoes, corncobs, half of the corn kernels, the stock, bay leaf, thyme, 1½ teaspoons salt, and ¼ teaspoon black pepper and stir to combine. Press the Cancel button to reset the program.

Lock the lid in place and turn the valve to Sealing. Press the Pressure Cook button and set the cook time for 15 minutes at high pressure.

Let the steam release naturally for 15 minutes, then turn the valve to Venting to quick-release any residual steam. Carefully remove the lid and discard the corncobs and bay leaf. Using an immersion blender (or transferring the soup in batches to a blender), purée the soup until smooth. Press the Cancel button to reset the program.

Press the Sauté button and bring the broth to a simmer. Add the milk, stir well, and simmer until well combined and hot, about 3 minutes. Add the remaining corn kernels and red pepper flakes (if using) and heat until the corn is cooked through, 2–3 minutes. Stir in the crabmeat. Taste and adjust the seasoning if needed.

Ladle the soup into bowls and top with the reserved bacon and parsley.

Red Curry Shrimp Soup

A few classic Thai ingredients—all of them easily found in Asian markets or well-stocked grocery stores—come together fast when cooked under pressure. Once the pressure is released, the shrimp cooks quickly in the hot liquid.

SERVES 4

4 cups (950 ml) chicken or vegetable stock (pages 124–125 or store-bought)

1 can (13½ fl oz/400 ml) full-fat coconut milk

2 tablespoons red curry paste

3 shallots, sliced

3 fresh or frozen Thai lime leaves

1 fresh red Thai chile, seeded and minced (optional)

1 clove garlic, minced

1 teaspoon peeled and grated fresh ginger

Kosher salt

1 package (8 oz/225 g) dried rice noodles

1 lb (450 g) shrimp, fresh or frozen, peeled and deveined

2 tablespoons fresh lime juice

FOR SERVING

Fresh basil leaves, preferably Thai

Combine the stock, coconut milk, curry paste, shallots, lime leaves, chile (if using), garlic, ginger, and 1 teaspoon salt in the Instant Pot® and stir to mix. Lock the lid in place and turn the valve to Sealing. Press the Pressure Cook button and set the cook time for 20 minutes at high pressure.

Meanwhile, cook the noodles according to the package directions and set aside.

Let the steam release naturally for 10 minutes, then turn the valve to Venting to quick-release any residual steam. Carefully remove the lid and discard the lime leaves. While the soup is still hot, add the shrimp to the pot and cook in the residual heat until pink and opaque, 2–3 minutes for fresh or about 4 minutes for frozen. Add the lime juice to the pot and stir to mix. Taste and adjust the seasoning as needed.

Divide the noodles evenly among four bowls and ladle the soup on top. Sprinkle each serving with a few basil leaves.

Tomato-Fennel Broth with Mussels

This broth, rich with fennel, garlic, white wine, and tomatoes, creates a simple yet satisfying base for nearly any type of seafood. Try peeled and deveined shrimp or 2-inch (5-cm) chunks of firm white fish in place of the mussels.

SERVES 4–6

1 tablespoon olive oil

1 tablespoon unsalted butter

2 fennel bulbs, stalks and fronds removed, sliced (reserve fronds for serving)

2 shallots, minced

6 cloves garlic, sliced

½ cup (120 ml) dry white wine

1 can (28 oz/800 g) whole tomatoes and their juice

3 cups (700 ml) chicken, vegetable, or fish stock (pages 124–126 or store-bought)

3 fresh oregano sprigs

1 bay leaf

Kosher salt and freshly ground black pepper

2 lb (1 kg) mussels, scrubbed and debearded

FOR THE PARSLEY OIL

½ cup (30 g) minced fresh flat-leaf parsley

Grated zest and juice of 1 lemon

¼ cup extra-virgin olive oil

1 clove garlic, minced

Select Sauté on the Instant Pot® and heat the olive oil and butter. Add the fennel and shallots and cook, stirring occasionally, until softened, about 5 minutes. Add the garlic and cook, stirring, until fragrant, about 1 minute. Add the wine and cook until almost completely absorbed, about 2 minutes. Add the tomatoes, breaking them up with a wooden spoon, then add the stock, oregano, bay leaf, 2 teaspoons salt, and ½ teaspoon pepper and stir to mix. Press the Cancel button to reset the program.

Lock the lid in place and turn the valve to Sealing. Press the Pressure Cook button and set the cook time for 10 minutes at high pressure.

Meanwhile, make the parsley oil. In a small bowl or glass measuring jug, whisk together the parsley, lemon zest and juice, oil, garlic, 1 teaspoon salt, and ¼ teaspoon pepper, mixing well (or combine the ingredients in a small lidded jar and shake well). Taste and adjust the seasoning if needed. Set aside.

Let the steam release naturally for 10 minutes, then turn the valve to Venting to quick-release any residual steam. Carefully remove the lid. Discard the bay leaf. Press the Cancel button to reset the program.

Press the Sauté button and add the mussels, discarding any that do not close to the touch. Cook until the mussels open, about 5 minutes. Discard any mussels that failed to open. Taste and adjust the seasoning if needed.

Ladle the soup into bowls and drizzle with parsley oil.

Smoky Seafood Chowder

This soup is a melting pot for whatever seafood you like. For example, you can swap out the clams for mussels—or use a combination of the two—or add sea or bay scallops with the white fish. The smoky flavor comes from both the bacon and the smoked salmon, but if you prefer, you can omit the bacon and cook the onion and celery in 2 tablespoons canola oil.

SERVES 6

2 slices thick-cut applewood-smoked bacon (about 2 oz/60 g total), chopped

1 yellow onion, chopped

2 ribs celery, sliced

1 cup (240 ml) white wine

1 lb (450 g) Yukon Gold potatoes, cut into 1-inch (2.5-cm) cubes

4 cups (950 ml) chicken, vegetable, or fish stock (pages 124–126 or store-bought)

Kosher salt and freshly ground black pepper

1 lb (450 g) clams, scrubbed

½ cup (120 ml) water

Select Sauté on the Instant Pot® three times to select Less mode and add the bacon. Cook, stirring occasionally, until the bacon is browned and most of the fat is rendered, about 5 minutes. Using a slotted spoon, transfer the bacon to a paper towel–lined plate.

Add the onion and celery to the pot and cook, stirring occasionally with a wooden spoon and scraping up any browned bits, until the vegetables are softened, about 5 minutes. Add ½ cup (120 ml) of the wine and cook for 1 minute. Press the Cancel button to reset the program.

Return the bacon to the pot and add the potatoes, stock, and 1 teaspoon salt. Lock the lid in place and turn the valve to Sealing. Press the Pressure Cook button and set the cook time for 7 minutes at high pressure.

Meanwhile, arrange the clams in a single layer in a medium sauté pan, discarding any that do not close to the touch, and pour in the remaining ½ cup (120 ml) wine and the water. Place over medium-low heat on the stove top, cover, and steam until the clams open, 5–10 minutes. Drain off the liquid and discard any clams that failed to open. Set aside.

Let the steam release naturally for 15 minutes, then turn the valve to Venting to quick-release any residual steam. Press the Cancel button to reset the program. Carefully remove the lid.

Press the Sauté button, add the fish and corn, and bring the broth to a simmer. Pour in the cream, stir gently, and simmer for 3 minutes. Press the Cancel button.

Add the salmon, cooked clams, and shrimp to the hot broth and heat until the salmon and clams are hot and the shrimp are pink and opaque, 2–3 minutes for fresh or about 4 minutes for frozen. Taste and adjust the seasoning if needed.

Ladle the chowder into bowls, top with chives and a few grindings of pepper, and serve with bread alongside.

1 lb (450 g) skinless thick white fish fillets, such as halibut or cod, cut into 2-inch (5-cm) pieces

1½ cups (250 g) fresh or frozen corn kernels

¾ cup (180 ml) heavy cream

½ lb (225 g) hot-smoked salmon, skinned and broken into 2-inch pieces

½ lb (225 g) shrimp, fresh or frozen, peeled and deveined

FOR SERVING

Chopped fresh chives, crusty bread

Coconut Fish Curry

The province of Goa, on the west coast of India, boasts a tropical cuisine that draws on both the Portuguese and the Indian pantries. Not surprisingly, seafood turns up in many dishes, including simple coconut milk–based curries like this one.

SERVES 4

1-inch (2.5-cm) piece fresh ginger, peeled

8 cloves garlic

½ cup (120 ml) water

1 tablespoon coconut or canola oil

1 yellow onion, chopped

2 fresh red Thai chiles, sliced and then seeded (for less heat) if desired

2 teaspoons ground cumin

1 teaspoon ground turmeric

2 cans (13½ fl oz/400 ml) full-fat coconut milk

2 cups (480 ml) chicken or vegetable stock (pages 124–125 or store-bought)

Kosher salt

1 red bell pepper, seeded and sliced

2 lb (1 kg) skinless firm white fish fillets, such as cod, halibut, or pollack, cut into 2-inch (5-cm) pieces

FOR SERVING

Steamed rice (page 128), optional; chopped fresh cilantro leaves

In a blender, combine the ginger, garlic, and water and blend until smooth.

Select Sauté on the Instant Pot® and heat the oil. Add the onion and cook, stirring occasionally, until softened, about 5 minutes. Add the ginger purée, chiles, cumin, and turmeric and cook, stirring, until well mixed, about 1 minute. Add the coconut milk, stock, and 1 teaspoon salt and stir to mix. Press the Cancel button to reset the program.

Lock the lid in place and turn the valve to Sealing. Press the Pressure Cook button and set the cook time for 10 minutes at high pressure.

Let the steam release naturally for 10 minutes, then turn the valve to Venting to quick-release any residual steam. Carefully remove the lid. Press the Cancel button to reset the program.

Press the Sauté button, add the bell pepper and fish, and cook until the pepper begins to soften and the fish is opaque when tested with a fork, about 5 minutes. Taste and adjust the seasoning with salt if needed.

Serve the curry in bowls, ladling it over rice, if using, and sprinkle with cilantro.

Ladle the soup over bowls of steamed white or brown rice for a more substantial meal.

Shrimp Jambalaya

You can never go wrong pairing Old Bay seasoning and nearly any seafood—and other foods as well. Here, the classic Maryland spice blend flavors shrimp and smoked sausage in a staple of the Creole table. For a fresh garnish, add a sprinkling of chopped fresh cilantro to each bowl at the table.

SERVES 4–6

2 tablespoons canola oil

1 large red bell pepper, seeded and coarsely chopped

1 large green bell pepper, seeded and coarsely chopped

1 large yellow onion, chopped

2 ribs celery, sliced

3 cloves garlic, minced

2½ teaspoons Old Bay seasoning

1 teaspoon garlic powder

½ teaspoon dried thyme

½ teaspoon smoked paprika

1½ cups long-grain white rice

2 tablespoons tomato paste

1 can (28 oz/800 g) crushed tomatoes and their juice

1½ cups (350 ml) chicken stock (page 124 or store-bought)

¾ lb (340 g) cooked smoked sausages, such as andouille, thinly sliced

Kosher salt and freshly ground black pepper

1 lb (450 g) shrimp, fresh or frozen, peeled and deveined

Select Sauté on the Instant Pot® and heat the oil. Add the bell peppers, onion, celery, and garlic and cook, stirring occasionally, until the vegetables start to soften, about 3 minutes. Add the Old Bay seasoning, garlic powder, thyme, and paprika and cook, stirring, until fragrant, about 1 minute. Add the rice, tomato paste, tomatoes, stock, sausages, 1 teaspoon salt, and ¼ teaspoon pepper and bring to a boil. Press the Cancel button to reset the program.

Lock the lid in place and turn the valve to Sealing. Press the Pressure Cook button and set the cook time for 8 minutes at high pressure.

Let the steam release naturally. Carefully remove the lid. Press the Sauté button and cook, stirring frequently, until slightly thickened, about 5 minutes. Add the shrimp and cook until pink and opaque, 2–3 minutes for fresh or about 4 minutes for frozen. Taste and adjust the seasoning if needed.

Ladle the jambalaya into bowls and serve.

New England Clam Chowder

In this easy breezy chowder, clam juice and canned chopped clams save time and work in the kitchen. For a thicker base, add a roux of flour and butter to the soup after pressure cooking and before adding the milk and cream (see note below). Oyster crackers are a traditional accompaniment.

SERVES 6

2 slices thick-cut bacon (about 2 oz/60 g total), chopped

1 yellow onion, chopped

2 ribs celery, sliced

3 fresh thyme sprigs, or ¼ teaspoon dried thyme

1 lb (450 g) russet potatoes (about 2 large), peeled and cut into 1-inch (2.5-cm) cubes

2 cans (6½ oz/185 g each) chopped clam meat, drained, with juice reserved

1 bottle (8 fl oz/240 ml) clam juice

2 cups (480 ml) water

Kosher salt and freshly ground black pepper

1½ cups (350 ml) whole milk

1 cup (240 ml) heavy cream

Pinch of cayenne pepper (optional)

FOR SERVING

Chopped fresh flat-leaf parsley, oyster crackers

Select Sauté on the Instant Pot® three times to select Less mode and add the bacon. Cook, stirring occasionally, until browned and most of the fat is rendered, about 5 minutes. Using a slotted spoon, transfer the bacon to a paper towel–lined plate. Add the onion and celery and cook, stirring occasionally and scraping up any browned bits, until softened, about 5 minutes. Add the thyme, potatoes, reserved clam juice, bottled clam juice, water, and 1 teaspoon salt and stir to mix. Press the Cancel button to reset the program.

Lock the lid in place and turn the valve to Sealing. Press the Pressure Cook button and set the cook time for 7 minutes at high pressure.

Let the steam release naturally for 15 minutes, then turn the valve to Venting to quick-release any residual steam. Carefully remove the lid and remove and discard the thyme sprigs, if used. Press the Cancel button to reset the program.

Press the Sauté button and bring the broth to a simmer. Add the milk and cream, stir to mix, and simmer until thoroughly combined and hot, about 3 minutes. Add the clam meat and cook until heated through, about 1 minute. Add the cayenne, if using, then taste and adjust the seasoning if needed.

Ladle the soup into bowls and top with parsley and the reserved bacon. Serve with oyster crackers alongside.

NOTE *To make a roux, heat 3 tablespoons butter in a small saucepan over medium-high heat. Add 3 tablespoons all-purpose flour and cook, stirring constantly, until a dark brown paste is formed, 15–20 minutes.*

For a bright finish, top each bowl with sliced fresh red Thai chiles and fresh cilantro leaves before serving.

Tom Yum with Shrimp

A classic soup of central Thailand, tom yum relies on a complex mix of spices, fish sauce, and other seasonings for its signature hot and sour flavor. Galangal is a tropical root with a distinctive lemon, cardamom, and ginger spiciness common in Thai, Indonesian, and Malaysian cooking. Ginger is the best substitute.

SERVES 4–6

2 stalks lemongrass, tough outer leaves and root end removed

2-inch (5-cm) piece fresh galangal or ginger, peeled and sliced

6 green Thai or 8 green serrano chiles, halved crosswise and seeded

3 cloves garlic

8 fresh or frozen Thai lime leaves

6 cups (1.4 L) chicken stock (page 124 or store-bought)

1 cup (100 g) fresh shimeji or oyster mushrooms, brushed clean, or drained canned straw mushrooms

4-inch (10-cm) piece bamboo shoot, thinly sliced, or 1 can (8 oz/227 g) sliced bamboo shoots, drained

1–2 tablespoons roasted chile paste

1 lb (450 g) shrimp, peeled and deveined

1–2 teaspoons coconut or granulated sugar

3–4 tablespoons fish sauce

Juice of 1–2 limes

To bruise the lemongrass, using the flat side of a chef's knife, push down firmly on each stalk until it splits open. Cut the stalks into 2-inch (5-cm) lengths.

Combine the lemongrass, galangal, chiles, garlic, 4 of the lime leaves, and the stock in the Instant Pot® and stir to mix.

Lock the lid in place and turn the valve to Sealing. Press the Pressure Cook button and set the cook time for 20 minutes at high pressure.

Let the steam release naturally, or for at least 15 minutes before turning the valve to Venting to quick-release any residual steam. Carefully remove the lid. Strain the broth through a colander set over a heatproof bowl. Press the Cancel button to reset the program.

Return the broth to the pot and press the Sauté button twice to select More mode. Add the mushrooms, bamboo shoots, and chile paste, stir well, and bring the broth to a boil. Add the shrimp and the remaining 4 lime leaves and cook until the shrimp turn pink and opaque, 2–3 minutes. Add 1 teaspoon of the sugar, 3 tablespoons of the fish sauce, and the juice of 1 lime and stir to mix. Taste and adjust the seasoning with more sugar, fish sauce, and lime juice if needed.

Ladle the soup into bowls and serve.

Crab Bisque

Substitute beef stock (page 125 or store-bought) for 1 cup (240 ml) of the fish stock for a richer flavor in this special occasion soup. Use cooked crabmeat from a fishmonger or from the refrigerated section of the grocery store.

SERVES 4

2 tablespoons unsalted butter

2 large shallots, chopped (about ¼ cup/35 g)

½ cup (120 ml) dry white wine

3 cups (700 ml) fish stock (page 126) or bottled clam juice

¼ cup (50 g) long-grain white rice

1 tablespoon tomato paste

Kosher salt

¾ lb (340 g) fresh lump crabmeat, picked over for shell fragments

1 cup (240 ml) heavy cream

⅛ teaspoon cayenne pepper

¼ cup (60 ml) dry sherry or Madeira (optional)

FOR SERVING

Chopped fresh flat-leaf parsley or chives, cayenne pepper (optional)

Select Sauté on the Instant Pot® and melt the butter. Add the shallots and cook, stirring occasionally, until softened, about 4 minutes. Add the wine and cook until absorbed, about 2 minutes. Add the stock, rice, tomato paste, and 1 teaspoon salt and stir to combine. Press the Cancel button to reset the program.

Lock the lid in place and turn the valve to Sealing. Press the Pressure Cook button and set the cook time for 10 minutes at high pressure.

Let the steam release naturally for 10 minutes, then turn the valve to Venting to quick-release any residual steam. Carefully remove the lid. Add ½ lb (225 g) of the crabmeat and stir to combine. Using an immersion blender (or transferring the soup in batches to a blender), purée the soup until smooth. Add the cream, cayenne, and sherry (if using) and stir until well mixed. Taste and adjust the seasoning if needed.

Ladle the soup into bowls and top with the remaining crabmeat, dividing it evenly. Top with parsley and sprinkle with cayenne, if using.

Mediterranean Fish Stew

You can vary the fish you choose for this Mediterranean-inspired seafood dish, selecting what looks freshest at the market. Tilapia, halibut, cod, or a combination would be delicious in the tomato-based broth.

SERVES 6

2 tablespoons olive oil

1 yellow onion, chopped

1 leek, halved lengthwise, rinsed well, and thinly sliced

½ fennel bulb, thinly sliced

4 cloves garlic, minced

1 can (28 oz/800 g) whole peeled tomatoes and their juice

2 cups (480 ml) fish stock (page 126) or bottled clam juice

2 cups (480 ml) water

1 bay leaf

2 pinches of saffron threads

¼ teaspoon red pepper flakes

1 teaspoon dried thyme

1 teaspoon grated orange zest

Kosher salt and freshly ground black pepper

1 lb (450 g) skinless white fish fillets (see note), cut into 2-inch (5-cm) pieces

1 lb (450 g) shrimp, fresh or frozen, peeled and deveined

FOR SERVING

Chopped fresh fennel fronds, chopped fresh flat-leaf parsley leaves, grilled crusty bread

Select Sauté on the Instant Pot® and heat the oil. Add the onion, leek, and fennel and cook, stirring occasionally, until softened, about 5 minutes. Add the garlic and tomatoes, breaking up the tomatoes with a wooden spoon. Cook, stirring occasionally, until combined, about 3 minutes. Add the stock, water, bay leaf, saffron, red pepper flakes, thyme, orange zest, 1 teaspoon salt, and ½ teaspoon black pepper and bring to a simmer, stirring occasionally. Press the Cancel button to reset the program.

Lock the lid in place and turn the valve to Sealing. Press the Pressure Cook button and set the cook time for 20 minutes at high pressure.

Let the steam release naturally, or for at least 15 minutes before turning the valve to Venting to quick-release any residual steam. Carefully remove the lid and discard the bay leaf. Press the Cancel button to reset the program.

Press the Sauté button, add the fish, and cook until opaque when tested with a fork, about 3 minutes. Add the shrimp and cook until they turn pink and opaque, 2–3 minutes for fresh or about 4 minutes for frozen. Taste and adjust the seasoning as needed.

Ladle the stew into bowls and top with fennel fronds, parsley, and pepper. Serve with bread alongside.

Chickpea, Chard & Coconut Curry Soup (page 119)

VEGETABLE

Coco-Tato

The catchy name of this easy vegan soup is as short as its list of ingredients. You can add to the list by wilting leafy greens—spinach, chard, kale—in the hot liquid after the pressure is released. To make a seafood variation, drop peeled and deveined shrimp into the hot soup and cook until they are pink and opaque.

SERVES 4–6

1 tablespoon canola oil

1 shallot, minced

3 cloves garlic, minced

2-inch (5-cm) piece fresh ginger, peeled and minced

2 cans (13½ fl oz/400 ml each) coconut milk

4 cups (950 ml) vegetable stock (page 125 or store-bought)

1 lb (450 g) Yukon Gold potatoes, cut into 2-inch (5-cm) cubes

Kosher salt

½ lb (225 g) green beans, trimmed and halved crosswise

1 red bell pepper, seeded and sliced

Juice of 1 lime

FOR SERVING

Fresh cilantro leaves, lime wedges

Select Sauté on the Instant Pot® and heat the oil. Add the shallot, garlic, and ginger and cook, stirring occasionally, until the shallot is translucent, 2–3 minutes. Add the coconut milk, stock, potatoes, and 1½ teaspoons salt and stir to combine. Press the Cancel button to reset the program.

Lock the lid in place and turn the valve to Sealing. Press the Pressure Cook button and set the cook time for 6 minutes at high pressure.

Let the steam release naturally for 15 minutes, then turn the valve to Venting to quick-release any residual steam. Carefully remove the lid. Press the Cancel button to reset the program.

Press the Sauté button. Add the beans and bell pepper, stir to combine, and cook until tender, about 4 minutes. Add the lime juice and stir to combine. Taste and adjust the seasoning as needed.

Ladle the soup into bowls, top with cilantro, and serve with lime wedges alongside.

A simple coconut broth studded with big chunks of potato creates the perfect canvas for a mix of colorful vegetables.

Butternut Squash Curry Soup

Sweet and satisfying butternut squash cubes cook in an ever-so-slightly spicy coconut broth in just 4 minutes, making this the perfect weeknight choice when saving time is top of mind. Although this soup doesn't need anything more, steamed white or brown rice (page 128) would be welcome alongside it.

SERVES 4

2 tablespoons canola or avocado oil

1 yellow onion, chopped

1 red bell pepper, seeded and sliced

3 tablespoons red curry paste

2 lb (1 kg) butternut squash, peeled, seeded, and cut into 1-inch (2.5-cm) cubes

1 can (13½ fl oz/400 ml) coconut milk

3 cups (700 ml) vegetable stock (page 125 or store-bought)

Kosher salt and freshly ground black pepper

FOR SERVING

Fresh basil leaves, preferably Thai

Select Sauté on the Instant Pot® and heat the oil. Add the onion and bell pepper and cook, stirring occasionally, until the vegetables start to soften, about 3 minutes. Add the curry paste and squash and stir until combined. Press the Cancel button to reset the program.

Add the coconut milk, stock, 1 teaspoon salt, and ¼ teaspoon pepper and stir to combine. Lock the lid in place and turn the valve to Sealing. Press the Pressure Cook button and set the cook time for 4 minutes at high pressure.

Turn the valve to Venting to quick-release the steam. Carefully remove the lid. Taste and adjust the seasoning if needed.

Ladle the soup into bowls and top with basil.

Purple Cauliflower & Mushroom

Mushrooms add umami, a base of rich, savory flavor, to dishes in which they are cooked. Their earthy taste and texture are a great match with mild, versatile cauliflower florets. To clean mushrooms, brush off the dirt gently with a kitchen towel. Don't dunk them into water, as they'll absorb it and won't brown as well.

SERVES 4

2 tablespoons unsalted butter

1 lb (450 g) cremini, portobello, chanterelle, or porcini mushrooms, or a combination, brushed clean and sliced

1 yellow onion, chopped

3 cloves garlic, minced

1 head purple or other cauliflower, cut into florets

4 cups (950 ml) chicken or vegetable stock (page 125 or store-bought)

4 fresh thyme sprigs

Kosher salt and freshly ground black pepper

½ cup (120 ml) heavy cream (optional)

2 tablespoons dry sherry (optional)

FOR SERVING

Toasted bread crumbs (page 130), optional

Select Sauté on the Instant Pot® and melt the butter. Add the mushrooms and cook, stirring occasionally, until they start to brown and release their liquid, about 5 minutes. Add the onion and garlic and cook, stirring occasionally, until the onion starts to soften, about 3 minutes. Add the cauliflower, stock, thyme, 2 teaspoons salt, and ¼ teaspoon pepper and stir to mix. Press the Cancel button to reset the program.

Lock the lid in place and turn the valve to Sealing. Press the Pressure Cook button and set the cook time for 20 minutes at high pressure.

Let the steam release naturally for 15 minutes, then turn the valve to Venting to quick-release any residual steam. Carefully remove the lid and discard the thyme sprigs. Using an immersion blender, blend the soup until smooth. (Alternatively, working in batches if necessary, transfer the soup to a blender and blend until smooth.) Stir in the cream and sherry, if using. Taste and adjust the seasoning if needed.

Ladle the soup into bowls and top with bread crumbs, if using.

Winter Root Vegetable Soup

This Irish-inspired hearty, healthy soup is ideal fare on a brisk winter's day. Use any combination of your favorite root vegetables, such as sweet potatoes, rutagabas, parsnips, celery roots, and/or turnips.

SERVES 6

3 tablespoons olive oil

½ yellow onion, chopped

2 leeks, white and pale green parts only, halved lengthwise, rinsed well, and sliced

2 ribs celery, sliced

3 cloves garlic, minced

1 tablespoon tomato paste

3 fresh oregano sprigs, or 1 teaspoon dried oregano

3 fresh thyme sprigs, or 1 teaspoon dried thyme

Kosher salt and freshly ground black pepper

2 carrots, peeled and sliced ½ inch (12 mm) thick

1½–2 lb (680 g–2 kg) assorted root vegetables (see note), cut into 2-inch (5-cm) cubes

1 lb (450 g) Yukon Gold potatoes, quartered

6 cups (1.4 L) chicken or vegetable stock (pages 124–125 or store-bought)

1 cup (30 g) spinach leaves or (65 g) chopped kale, or Swiss chard (optional)

Chopped fresh flat-leaf parsley leaves

Select Sauté on the Instant Pot® and heat the oil. Add the onion, leeks, and celery and cook, stirring occasionally, until softened, about 5 minutes. Add the garlic and cook, stirring, until fragrant, about 1 minute. Add the tomato paste, oregano, thyme, 2 teaspoons salt, and ½ teaspoon pepper and stir to mix. Add the carrots, root vegetables, potatoes, and stock and again stir until combined. Press the Cancel button to reset the program.

Lock the lid in place and turn the valve to Sealing. Press the Pressure Cook button and set the cook time for 5 minutes at high pressure.

Let the steam release naturally for 10 minutes, then turn the valve to Venting to quick-release any residual steam. Carefully remove the lid and discard the herb sprigs (if used). Immediately add the spinach, kale, or chard and stir to mix. The spinach will wilt in the hot liquid in about 1 minute and the kale or chard in about 2 minutes. Taste and adjust the seasoning if needed.

Ladle the soup into bowls and top with parsley.

Green Garlic & Coconut

Green garlic, which has long, tender leaves, a small bulb, and a mild flavor, is garlic that is harvested in spring before the bulb matures. When you see it in the market, make this creamy take on potato soup and freeze some for enjoying later in the year.

SERVES 4–6

1 stalk lemongrass, tough outer leaves and root end removed

6 green garlic bulbs (about 1½ lb/680 g total), quartered, green tops reserved for serving

1 lb (450 g) russet potatoes, peeled and cut into 2-inch (5-cm) cubes

1 can (13½ fl oz/400 ml) coconut milk

4 cups (950 ml) chicken or vegetable stock (pages 124–125 or store-bought)

Kosher salt

1 teaspoon sugar

Juice of 1 lime

FOR SERVING

Sliced green garlic tops, sliced green onions

To bruise the lemongrass, using the flat side of a chef's knife, push down firmly on the stalk until it splits open. Cut the stalk into 3-inch (7.5-cm) lengths.

Put the lemongrass, garlic bulbs, potatoes, coconut milk, stock, and 1 teaspoon salt into the Instant Pot® and stir to mix. Lock the lid in place and turn the valve to Sealing. Press the Pressure Cook button and set the cook time for 10 minutes at high pressure.

Let the pressure release naturally for 15 minutes, then turn the valve to Venting to quick-release any residual steam. Carefully remove the lid and remove and discard the lemongrass. Using an immersion blender, blend the soup until smooth. (Alternatively, transfer the soup to a blender and blend until smooth, working in batches if necessary.) Stir in the sugar and half the lime juice. Taste and adjust the seasoning, adding more lime juice as needed.

To serve, ladle into bowls and top with sliced green garlic tops and green onions.

Pasta e Fagioli

The main components of this soup are prepared in two stages—an initial, longer cooking time for the dried beans, followed by a quick second round of pressure cooking for the pasta. Don't skimp on the parsley. It adds a welcome fresh taste to this hearty bowl.

SERVES 6

2 tablespoons olive oil

2 yellow onions, chopped

2 tablespoons minced garlic

¼ lb (115 g) pancetta, chopped

1 can (14½ oz/410 g) diced tomatoes and their juice

1 cup (200 g) dried cannellini beans, picked over and rinsed

6 cups (1.4 L) chicken or beef stock (pages 124–125 or store-bought)

2 tablespoons minced fresh oregano

Kosher salt and freshly ground black pepper

1 cup (½ lb/225 g) dried pennette, ditalini, macaroni, or tubettini pasta

¼ cup (15 g) minced fresh flat-leaf parsley

FOR SERVING

Minced fresh flat-leaf parsley

Select Sauté on the Instant Pot® and heat the oil. Add the onions and cook, stirring occasionally, until very soft and tender, about 8 minutes. Add the garlic and cook, stirring, until fragrant, 1 minute. Add the pancetta and cook, stirring occasionally, until starting to brown, about 5 minutes. Add the tomatoes, beans, stock, oregano, 1½ teaspoons salt, and ¼ teaspoon pepper and stir to mix. Press Cancel to reset the program.

Lock the lid in place and turn the valve to Sealing. Press the Pressure Cook button and set the cook time for 35 minutes at high pressure.

Let the steam release naturally for 10 minutes, then turn the valve to Venting to quick-release any residual steam. Carefully remove the lid, add the pasta, and stir to mix. Lock the lid in place and turn the valve to Sealing. Press the Pressure Cook button and set the cook time for 2 minutes at high pressure. (Alternatively, you can skip the second pressure cooking step and cook the pasta on Sauté mode until it starts to soften, about 6 minutes. The pasta will continue to soften as it sits in the hot liquid.)

Turn the valve to Venting to quick-release the steam. Carefully remove the lid. Stir in the parsley and taste and adjust the seasoning if needed.

Ladle into bowls and top with parsley.

Rainbow Minestrone

This everything-but-the-kitchen-sink soup is flavorful, colorful, and versatile. Use other vegetables in season, if you like, cooking hearty ones under pressure and adding more delicate ones to the hot liquid after the pressure is released.

SERVES 6

2 tablespoons unsalted butter

1 yellow onion, chopped

2 carrots, peeled, halved lengthwise, and cut into half-moons ¼ inch (6 mm) thick

2 ribs celery, sliced

2 cloves garlic, minced

½ lb (225 g) small waxy potatoes in assorted colors, halved

1 can (15 oz/425 g) diced tomatoes and their juice

4 cups (950 ml) chicken stock (page 124 or store-bought)

4 cups (950 ml) water

1 cup (200 g) dried white beans, picked over and rinsed

3 fresh oregano sprigs

1 large piece Parmesan cheese rind (optional)

1 cup (100 g) dried ditalini, tubetti, macaroni, or other small pasta

1 bunch kale or other hearty green, stemmed and coarsely chopped

½ lb (225 g) summer squash, cut into small cubes

FOR SERVING

Freshly grated Parmesan cheese, fresh basil leaves

Select Sauté on the Instant Pot® and melt the butter. Add the onion and cook, stirring occasionally, until softened and translucent, about 5 minutes. Add the carrots and celery and cook, stirring occasionally, until they start to soften, about 3 minutes. Add the garlic and cook, stirring, until fragrant, about 1 minute. Add the potatoes, tomatoes, stock, water, beans, oregano, Parmesan rind (if using), 1½ teaspoons salt, and ¼ teaspoon pepper and stir to mix. Press the Cancel button to reset the program.

Lock the lid in place and turn the valve to Sealing. Press the Pressure Cook button and set the cook time for 30 minutes at high pressure.

Let the steam release naturally for 15 minutes, then turn the valve to Venting to quick-release any residual steam. Press the Cancel button to reset the program. Carefully remove the lid.

Add the pasta and stir to combine. Lock the lid in place and turn the valve to Sealing. Press the Pressure Cook button and set the cook time for 2 minutes at high pressure.

Turn the valve to Venting to quick-release the steam. Carefully remove the lid and discard the cheese rind. Immediately add the kale and zucchini and stir to mix. The kale will wilt and the zucchini will soften in 3–5 minutes. Taste and adjust the seasoning if needed.

Ladle the soup into bowls and top with cheese and basil.

Sweet Potato-Lemongrass

This super-simple vegan soup gets its bright flavor from lemongrass and its creaminess from coconut milk. Before dropping the lemongrass into the pot, be sure to give it a good bruising with a knife—a meat mallet or pestle will work too—to release its citrusy fragrance.

SERVES 4–6

2 stalks lemongrass, tough outer leaves and root end removed

2 tablespoons unsalted butter

1 yellow onion, chopped

2 cloves garlic, crushed

2 lb (1 kg) sweet potatoes, peeled and cut into 1-inch cubes

3 cups (700 ml) chicken or vegetable stock (pages 124–125 or store-bought)

1 can (13½ fl oz/400 ml) coconut milk

Kosher salt and freshly ground black pepper

FOR SERVING

Fresh cilantro leaves, lime wedges

To bruise the lemongrass, using the flat side of a chef's knife, push down firmly on each stalk until it splits open. Cut the stalks into 2-inch (5-cm) lengths.

Select Sauté on the Instant Pot® and melt the butter. Add the onion and cook, stirring occasionally, until softened, about 5 minutes. Add the garlic and cook, stirring, until fragrant, about 1 minute. Add the sweet potatoes, stock, coconut milk, lemongrass, 1 teaspoon salt, and ¼ teaspoon pepper and stir to combine. Press the Cancel button to reset the program.

Lock the lid in place and turn the valve to Sealing. Press the Pressure Cook button and set the cook time for 10 minutes at high pressure.

Let the steam release naturally for 10 minutes, then turn the valve to Venting to quick-release any residual steam. Carefully remove the lid and discard the lemongrass. Using an immersion blender (or transferring the soup in batches to a blender), purée the soup until smooth. Taste and adjust the seasoning if needed.

Ladle the soup into bowls, top with cilantro, and serve with lime wedges alongside.

Hearty Vegetable with Brown Rice

During the summer months, when fresh tomatoes and corn are in season, use them in place of the canned tomatoes (about 2 pounds/1 kg fresh tomatoes) and frozen corn to take this chunky, good-for-you soup to the next level. A generous garnish of chopped basil heightens the rich mix of flavors in this vegetarian soup.

SERVES 4–6

2 tablespoons olive oil

1 yellow onion, chopped

5 cloves garlic, minced

1 can (28 oz/800 g) whole tomatoes with their juice

1 teaspoon dried oregano

Kosher salt and freshly ground black pepper

4 cups (950 ml) vegetable stock (page 125 or store-bought)

1 cup (200 g) long-grain brown rice

2 zucchini, cut into small cubes

1 cup (170 g) fresh or frozen corn kernels (about 2 ears)

2 cups (60 g) baby spinach

FOR SERVING
Chopped fresh basil leaves

Select Sauté on the Instant Pot® and heat the oil. Add the onion and cook, stirring occasionally, until softened, about 5 minutes. Add the garlic and cook, stirring, until fragrant, 1 minute. Add the tomatoes, breaking them up with a wooden spoon, then add the oregano, 2 teaspoons salt, and ½ teaspoon pepper and cook for 1 minute. Press the Cancel button to reset the program.

Add the stock and rice to the pot and stir to combine. Lock the lid in place and turn the valve to Sealing. Press the Pressure Cook button and set the cook time for 15 minutes at high pressure.

Let the steam release naturally, or for at least 15 minutes before turning the valve to Venting to quick-release any residual steam. Carefully remove the lid. Immediately add the zucchini, corn, and spinach, stir to mix, and cook until the corn and zucchini are heated through and the spinach is wilted, about 2 minutes. Taste and adjust the seasoning if needed.

Ladle the soup into bowls and sprinkle with basil.

Lentil & Vegetable Dal

This fully loaded Indian comfort meal boasts a texture trifecta—firm rice, creamy dal, and soft naan. If purple, yellow, or green cauliflower is in the market, use it in place of the common white head for extra color. And don't skip the butter. It adds a rich, creamy finish.

SERVES 6

3 cloves garlic, minced

1-inch (2.5-cm) piece fresh ginger, peeled and grated

1 tablespoon ground coriander

1 teaspoon ground cumin

¼ teaspoon cayenne pepper

¼ teaspoon ground turmeric

3 tablespoons grapeseed or coconut oil

2 cups (200 g) bite-size cauliflower florets

Kosher salt

4 cups (950 ml) plus 2 tablespoons water

1 yellow onion, chopped

1 cup (about 225 g) puréed or finely chopped tomatoes

1 cup (200 g) black lentils

2 tablespoons unsalted butter

FOR SERVING

Steamed rice (page 128), chopped fresh cilantro leaves, warmed naan, plain yogurt (optional)

In a small bowl, combine the garlic, ginger, coriander, cumin, cayenne, and turmeric and stir to mix.

Select Sauté on the Instant Pot® and heat 1 tablespoon of the oil. Add the cauliflower and ½ teaspoon salt, stir to mix, and cook for 1 minute. Add the 2 tablespoons water and cook, stirring occasionally, until the cauliflower begins to soften, about 5 minutes. Transfer the cauliflower to a plate.

Heat the remaining 2 tablespoons oil in the pot, add the onion, and cook, stirring occasionally, until softened, about 3 minutes. Add the garlic mixture, stir to mix, and cook for about 1 minute. Add the tomatoes, stir to mix, and cook for 1 minute. Press the Cancel button to reset the program.

Add the lentils, the 4 cups (950 ml) water, and 1 teaspoon salt to the pot and stir to mix. Lock the lid in place and turn the valve to Sealing. Press the Pressure Cook button and set the cook time for 15 minutes at high pressure.

Let the steam release naturally. Carefully remove the lid, return the cauliflower to the pot, and stir to mix well and warm through. Stir in the butter until melted. Taste and adjust with salt as needed.

Spoon the dal over rice in individual bowls and sprinkle with cilantro. Serve with naan and yogurt alongside, if desired.

Mexican Black Bean Soup

Smoky, spicy, and smooth, this robust vegetarian soup gets an extra kick of flavor from a tangy lime crema that's spooned on top just before serving. Serve with tortilla chips and chopped fresh cilantro leaves for diners to add at the table.

SERVES 6

1 tablespoon canola oil

1 yellow onion, diced

1 red bell pepper, seeded and diced

1 jalapeño chile, seeded and minced

3 cloves garlic, minced

1 tablespoon adobo sauce from canned chipotle chiles

1 tablespoon ground cumin

1½ teaspoons smoked paprika

1 teaspoon dried oregano

Kosher salt and freshly ground black pepper

2¼ cups (1 lb/450 g) dried black beans, picked over and rinsed

4 cups (950 ml) vegetable stock (page 125 or store-bought)

1 tablespoon fresh lime juice

FOR THE CREMA

1 cup (225 g) sour cream

¼ cup (15 g) chopped fresh cilantro

¼ cup (40 g) minced red onion

1 tablespoon fresh lime juice

1 teaspoon grated lime zest

Select Sauté on the Instant Pot® and heat the oil. Add the yellow onion and bell pepper and cook, stirring occasionally, until softened, about 5 minutes. Add the jalapeño, garlic, adobo sauce, cumin, paprika, oregano, and 1 teaspoon salt and cook, stirring occasionally, until fragrant, about 2 minutes. Add the beans and stock and stir to mix. Press the Cancel button to reset the program.

Lock the lid in place and turn the valve to Sealing. Press the Pressure Cook button and set the cook time for 45 minutes at high pressure.

While the soup cooks, make the crema. In a small bowl, combine the sour cream, cilantro, red onion, lime juice and zest, ½ teaspoon salt, and a few grindings of pepper and stir to mix. Taste and adjust the seasoning as needed.

When the soup has finished cooking, let the steam release naturally for 15 minutes, then turn the valve to Venting to quick-release any residual steam. Carefully remove the lid. Stir in the lime juice and a few grindings of pepper. Taste and adjust the seasoning as needed.

Ladle the soup into bowls and top each serving with a large spoonful of the crema.

Rustic Beans & Greens

Choose the type of dried beans and leafy greens you like best for this vegetarian soup. If you opt for navy beans or red kidney beans, reduce the cooking time to 25 minutes. Tuscan or curly kale, Swiss chard, and/or collard greens all work well.

SERVES 6

2 tablespoons olive oil

1 yellow onion, chopped

2 carrots, peeled and chopped

2 ribs celery, sliced

4 cloves garlic, minced

1 can (15 oz/425 g) diced tomatoes and their juice

1 teaspoon dried oregano

¼ teaspoon red pepper flakes

Kosher salt and freshly ground black pepper

4 cups (950 ml) vegetable stock (page 125 or store-bought)

1 cup (200 g) dried cannellini beans, chickpeas, or a mix, picked over and rinsed

1 bay leaf

1 large piece Parmesan cheese rind (optional)

1 cup (240 ml) water

¾ lb (340 g) leafy greens (see note), stemmed and chopped (about 4 cups/150 g)

FOR SERVING

Chopped fresh flat-leaf parsley leaves, freshly grated Parmesan cheese

Select Sauté on the Instant Pot® and heat the oil. Add the onion, carrots, and celery and cook, stirring occasionally, until softened, about 5 minutes. Add the garlic and cook, stirring, until fragrant, 1 minute. Add the tomatoes, oregano, red pepper flakes, 2 teaspoons salt, and ½ teaspoon pepper and cook, stirring, for about 1 minute to blend well. Press the Cancel button to reset the program.

Add the stock, beans, bay leaf, Parmesan rind (if using), and water to the pot and stir to mix. Lock the lid in place and turn the valve to Sealing. Press the Pressure Cook button and set the cook time for 40 minutes at high pressure.

Let the steam release naturally, or for at least 15 minutes before turning the valve to Venting to quick-release any residual steam. Carefully remove the lid and discard the bay leaf and Parmesan rind. Immediately add the greens and stir to mix. The greens will wilt in the hot liquid in 3–5 minutes, depending on the type of green. Taste and adjust the seasoning as needed.

Ladle the soup into bowls and sprinkle with parsley and cheese.

French Onion Soup

Make sure to use flameproof bowls or crocks for this classic soup. Porcelain holds heat well and stands up to the direct heat of the broiler, which melts the delicious cheese on top in just a few minutes. Gruyère cheese is traditional, but Swiss, Emmentaler, or Comté can be substituted.

SERVES 4

1 tablespoon olive oil

2 tablespoons unsalted butter

1½ lb (680 g) yellow onions, sliced lengthwise

1 teaspoon sugar

¼ teaspoon baking powder

1 teaspoon all-purpose flour

¼ cup (60 ml) dry white wine

4 cups (950 ml) beef or chicken stock (pages 124–125 or store-bought)

1 tablespoon molasses

3 fresh thyme sprigs, or 1 teaspoon dried thyme

1 bay leaf

Kosher salt and freshly ground black pepper

3 tablespoons Cognac or dry sherry (optional)

FOR SERVING

Baguette, sliced 1 inch (2.5 m) thick (8–12 slices); shredded Gruyère or Swiss cheese

Select Sauté on the Instant Pot® and heat the oil and melt the butter. Press the Sauté button again to select the More mode. Add the onions, sugar, and baking powder and cook, stirring often, until the onions are evenly golden brown, 25–30 minutes. Add the flour and stir to coat the onions well. Add the wine, stirring to scrape up any browned bits, and then add ¼ cup (60 ml) of the stock, continuing to scrape up any browned bits. Add the remaining stock, the molasses, thyme, bay leaf, and 1 teaspoon salt and stir to mix. Press the Cancel button to reset the program.

Lock the lid in place and turn the valve to Sealing. Press the Pressure Cook button and set the cook time for 8 minutes at high pressure.

Let the steam release naturally for 15 minutes, then turn the valve to Venting to quick-release any residual steam. Meanwhile, preheat the broiler. When the steam is fully released, carefully remove the lid and discard the thyme sprigs and bay leaf. Add the cognac, if using, and stir to mix. Taste and adjust the seasoning if needed.

Place four heatproof serving bowls on a heavy-duty sheet pan and ladle the soup into the bowls. Place 2–3 baguette slices on top of each bowl. Generously sprinkle cheese on the bread slices. Place the pan under the broiler about 4 inches (10 cm) from the heat source and broil until the cheese melts and starts to turn golden brown, 4–5 minutes. Serve right away.

For a vegetarian version of this French classic, substitute vegetable stock (page 125 or store-bought) for the beef stock.

Spiced Carrot & Cashew

You'll likely have many of the pantry and fridge staples needed for this creamy soup on hand, but a dollop of crème fraîche and a sprinkling of tarragon add a luxe finishing touch you won't want to miss. You can also dust each bowl with a pinch of smoked paprika for a bit of smoky, sweet flavor.

SERVES 6

3 tablespoons olive oil

6 carrots, peeled and chopped

2 ribs celery, chopped

1 yellow onion, chopped

2 cloves garlic, minced

2 teaspoons curry powder

1 teaspoon smoked paprika

¾ teaspoon ground cumin

½ teaspoon chili powder

½ teaspoon ground ginger

Pinch of cayenne pepper

Kosher salt and freshly ground black pepper

2 cups (225 g) unsalted raw cashews

1 bay leaf

4 cups (950 ml) chicken or vegetable stock (pages 124–125 or store-bought)

2 teaspoons grated orange zest

FOR SERVING

Crème fraîche, fresh tarragon leaves, chopped toasted almonds

Select Sauté on the Instant Pot® and heat the oil. Add the carrots, celery, and onion and cook, stirring occasionally, until the vegetables begin to brown, about 5 minutes. Add the garlic, curry powder, paprika, cumin, chili powder, ginger, and cayenne, season with salt and pepper, and continue to cook, stirring occasionally, until the vegetables are well coated with the spices, about 5 minutes. Add the cashews, bay leaf, and stock and stir to mix. Press the Cancel button to reset the program.

Lock the lid in place and turn the valve to Sealing. Press the Soup button and set the cook time for 20 minutes at high pressure.

Turn the valve to Venting to quick-release the steam. Carefully remove the lid. Using an immersion blender (or transferring the soup in batches to a blender), purée the soup until smooth. Stir in the orange zest. Taste and adjust the seasoning with salt and black pepper.

Ladle the soup into bowls and top with crème fraîche, tarragon, and almonds.

Spicy Tomato Soup with Toasted Bread Crumbs

Here's a great way to use up imperfect or very ripe tomatoes at the height of the tomato season. For a popular, kid-friendly rendition, omit the cayenne pepper and trade out the toasted bread crumbs for grilled cheese cut into small squares. Chopped fresh parsley or chives can stand in for the dill.

SERVES 4–6

1 tablespoon olive oil

1 yellow onion, chopped

1 carrot, peeled and chopped

4 cloves garlic, minced

½ teaspoon cayenne pepper

3 lb (1.4 kg) tomatoes, seeded and chopped

1½ cups (350 ml) chicken or vegetable stock (pages 124–125 or store-bought)

Kosher salt and freshly ground black pepper

Pinch of sugar

FOR SERVING

Toasted bread crumbs (page 130), chopped fresh dill

Select Sauté on the Instant Pot® and heat the oil. Add the onion and carrot and cook, stirring occasionally, until softened, about 5 minutes. Add the garlic and cayenne pepper and cook, stirring, until fragrant, about 1 minute. Add the tomatoes, stock, 2 teaspoons salt, and ½ teaspoon pepper and stir to mix. Press the Cancel button to reset the program.

Lock the lid in place and turn the valve to Sealing. Press the Pressure Cook button and set the cook time for 20 minutes at high pressure.

Let the steam release naturally for 15 minutes, then turn the valve to Venting to quick-release any residual steam. Carefully remove the lid. Using an immersion blender (or transferring the soup in batches to a blender), purée the soup until smooth. Stir in the sugar. Taste and adjust the seasoning if needed.

Ladle the soup into bowls and top with bread crumbs and dill.

Embellish each bowl with leaves of fresh Thai basil and fresh cilantro for a boost of crisp, clean flavor.

Thai Pumpkin Green Curry with Noodles

Pumpkin takes the place of meat in this cozy curry. If it's not in the market, kabocha or acorn squash can be substituted. Flat, wide rice noodles are the best match for the large chunks of pumpkin, but any long, wide noodle will work in a pinch. Don't leave off the herb toppings, as they brighten the rich sauce.

SERVES 4–6

2–2½ lb (1–1.1 kg) pumpkin

1 stalk lemongrass, tough outer leaves and root end removed

1 tablespoon coconut or canola oil

2 small or 1 large shallot, minced

2 green Thai chiles, seeded if desired (for less heat) and chopped

4 cloves garlic, minced

2-inch (5-cm) piece fresh ginger, peeled and minced

3 tablespoons Thai green curry paste

2 cups (480 ml) chicken or vegetable stock (pages 124–125 or store-bought)

2 cans (13½ fl oz/400 ml each) coconut milk

8 fresh or frozen Thai lime leaves

1 package (8 oz/225 g) flat, wide rice or wheat noodles

Handful of fresh Thai basil leaves

2–3 tablespoons fish sauce

1–2 teaspoons granulated sugar

Juice of 1–2 limes

Cut the pumpkin in half, remove the seeds, then cut away the peel and discard. Cut the flesh into 2-inch (5-cm) cubes. To bruise the lemongrass, using the flat side of a chef's knife, push down firmly on the stalk until it splits open. Cut the stalk in half crosswise.

Select Sauté on the Instant Pot® and heat the oil. Add the shallots, chiles, garlic, and ginger and cook, stirring occasionally, until softened and fragrant, about 2 minutes. Add the curry paste and stir until mixed. Add the stock, coconut milk, pumpkin, lemongrass, and lime leaves and again stir until mixed. Press the Cancel button to reset the program.

Lock the lid in place and turn the valve to Sealing. Press the Pressure Cook button and set the cook time for 5 minutes at high pressure.

Meanwhile, cook the noodles according to the package directions and set aside.

Let the steam release naturally for 5 minutes, then turn the valve to Venting to quick-release any residual steam. Carefully remove the lid and discard the lemongrass and lime leaves. Add the basil, 2 tablespoons of the fish sauce, 1 teaspoon of the sugar, and the juice of 1 lime and stir to mix. Taste and adjust the seasoning with more lime juice, sugar, and fish sauce if needed.

Divide the noodles evenly among individual serving bowls. Ladle the curry over the noodles and serve.

Butternut Squash-Apple Purée

This recipe yields a good-size batch of soup, making it an ideal choice when planning a casual fall dinner for friends. If you're pressed for time, look for precut butternut squash chunks in the produce section at the grocery store.

SERVES 6–8

1 tablespoon olive oil

1 large leek, white and pale green parts only, halved lengthwise, rinsed well, and sliced

4 cloves garlic, minced

2 tablespoons chopped fresh sage

2 teaspoons ground cumin

4 lb (1.8 kg) butternut squash, peeled, seeded, and cut into 2-inch (5-cm) chunks, or 2½ lb (1.1 kg) prepared butternut squash chunks

1 lb (450 g) tart apples, such as Granny Smith, peeled, quartered, and cored

1 cup (240 ml) hard cider or dry white wine

4 cups (950 ml) chicken or vegetable stock (pages 124–125 or store-bought)

Kosher salt and freshly ground black pepper

FOR SERVING

½ cup (115 g) crème fraîche (optional), crusty bread

Select Sauté on the Instant Pot® and heat the oil. Add the leek and cook, stirring occasionally, until softened, about 5 minutes. Add the garlic, sage, and cumin and cook, stirring, until fragrant, about 1 minute. Add the squash and apples and cook, stirring occasionally, until they start to soften, about 3 minutes. Add the cider and cook until it is almost completely absorbed, about 2 minutes. Press the Cancel button to reset the program.

Add the stock, 2 teaspoons salt, and ¼ teaspoon pepper and stir to mix. Lock the lid in place and turn the valve to Sealing. Press the Pressure Cook button and set the cook time for 20 minutes at high pressure.

Let the steam release naturally for 10 minutes, then turn the valve to Venting to quick-release any residual steam. Carefully remove the lid. Using an immersion blender (or transferring the soup in batches to a blender), purée the soup until smooth. Taste and adjust the seasoning if needed.

Ladle the soup into bowls and top each serving with a dollop of crème fraîche, if using. Serve with bread alongside.

Cauliflower Cheddar Ale Soup

Warm up on a cold fall day with this sweet and nutty country-style soup. Stick to a brown or amber ale for the best flavor (hoppy beers can be bitter), and don't forget the big, thick slices of country bread for dunking.

SERVES 6–8

2 lb (1 kg) cauliflower florets

1 large yellow onion, chopped

2 large carrots, peeled and chopped

3 ribs celery, sliced

4 cups (950 ml) chicken or vegetable stock (pages 124–125 or store-bought)

1 bottle (12 fl oz/354 ml) brown or amber ale

2 tablespoons Worcestershire sauce

1 tablespoon Dijon mustard

2 bay leaves

Kosher salt and freshly ground black pepper

10 oz (285 g) sharp white Cheddar cheese, shredded (about 2½ cups)

FOR SERVING

Thick slices country bread

Combine the cauliflower, onion, carrots, celery, stock, ale, Worcestershire sauce, mustard, bay leaves, and 2 teaspoons salt In the Instant Pot® and stir to mix.

Lock the lid in place and turn the valve to Sealing. Press the Pressure Cook button and set the cook time for 10 minutes at high pressure.

Let the steam release naturally, or for at least 15 minutes before turning the valve to Venting to quick-release any residual steam. Carefully remove the lid and discard the bay leaves. Using an immersion blender (or transferring the soup to a blender in batches), purée the soup until smooth. Immediately stir in the cheese until it melts. Season with pepper, then taste and adjust the seasoning if needed.

Ladle the soup into bowls and serve with bread alongside.

Carrot-Ginger Soup with Turmeric

Brightly colored and refreshing, this flavorful take on carrot soup departs from more typical recipes by adding fresh and ground ginger and turmeric. A sprinkling of toasted pepitas and smoked paprika when serving adds crunch and punch to a juice bar–inspired ingredient combo.

SERVES 4–6

2 tablespoons unsalted butter

1 yellow onion, chopped

2 cloves garlic, minced

2 lb (1 kg) carrots, peeled and sliced ½ inch (12 mm) thick

½ teaspoon ground turmeric

½ teaspoon ground ginger

Kosher salt and freshly ground black pepper

4 cups (950 ml) chicken or vegetable stock (pages 124–125 or store-bought)

1 tablespoon peeled and grated fresh ginger

½ cup (120 ml) orange juice, preferably fresh

FOR SERVING (OPTIONAL)

Toasted pepitas, smoked paprika

Select Sauté on the Instant Pot® and melt the butter. Add the onion and cook, stirring occasionally, until softened, about 5 minutes. Add the garlic and cook, stirring, until fragrant, about 1 minute. Add the carrots, turmeric, ground ginger, 1½ teaspoons salt, and ¼ teaspoon pepper and stir to mix. Press the Cancel button to reset the program.

Add the stock, fresh ginger, and orange juice and stir to mix. Lock the lid in place and turn the valve to Sealing. Press the Pressure Cook button and set the cook time for 15 minutes at high pressure.

Let the steam release naturally for 15 minutes, then turn the valve to Venting to quick-release any residual steam. Carefully remove the lid. Using an immersion blender (or transferring the soup in batches to a blender), purée the soup until smooth. Taste and adjust the seasoning if needed.

Ladle the soup into bowls. Top with toasted pepitas and sprinkle with smoked paprika, if desired.

Toasted pepitas and a light sprinkling of smoked paprika make a vibrant garnish.

Split Pea

Here's a fun fact: dried peas contain about triple the amount of protein of fresh peas by volume. To enhance the flavor of this protein-packed favorite, add ½ pound (225 g) whole andouille sausages when cooking the soup, remove them just before puréeing, slice them, and return the slices to the pot at the end.

SERVES 4–6

1 tablespoon olive oil

1 large leek, white and pale green parts only, halved lengthwise, rinsed well, and sliced

1 carrot, peeled and chopped

1 rib celery, chopped

3 tomatoes, seeded and coarsely chopped, or 1 cup (170 g) canned diced tomatoes

6 cups (1.4 L) chicken stock (page 124 or store-bought) or water

1½ cups (300 g) dried split peas, picked over and rinsed

Kosher salt and freshly ground black pepper

3 fresh flat-leaf parsley sprigs

3 fresh thyme sprigs

1 bay leaf

2 orange peel strips, each 2 inches (5 cm) long by 1 inch (2.5 cm) wide and stuck with 1 whole clove

Select Sauté on the Instant Pot® and heat the oil. Add the leek and cook, stirring occasionally, until it begins to wilt, about 3 minutes. Add the carrot and celery and cook, stirring occasionally, until they start to soften, about 3 minutes. Add the tomatoes, stock, split peas, and 1 teaspoon salt and stir to mix. Press the Cancel button to reset the program.

Gather the parsley and thyme sprigs, bay leaf, and orange peel strips into a bunch, fold over the stems, and tie securely with kitchen twine to form a bouquet garni (or wrap them in a piece of cheesecloth and secure with twine; see page 48). Add to the pot. Lock the lid in place and turn the valve to Sealing. Press the Pressure Cook button and set the cook time for 20 minutes at high pressure.

Let the steam release naturally for 15 minutes, then turn the valve to Venting to quick-release any residual steam. Carefully remove the lid and discard the bouquet garni. Using an immersion blender (or transferring the soup in batches to a blender), purée the soup until smooth. Season with pepper, then taste and adjust the seasoning if needed.

Ladle the soup into bowls and serve.

Potato-Leek

Just four main ingredients—leeks, stock, potatoes, and cream—make this classic soup even easier to prepare in an Instant Pot®. It's a great first course for dinner or the perfect partner for a salad at lunch or brunch. A touch of cream at the end creates a silky finish, but you can leave it out if you prefer a dairy-free vegan dish.

SERVES 4–6

1 tablespoon olive oil

2 leeks, white and pale green parts only, halved lengthwise, rinsed well, and sliced

4 cups (950 ml) chicken or vegetable stock (pages 124–125 or store-bought)

2 russet potatoes (about 1½ lb/680 g total), peeled and cut into 2-inch (5-cm)cubes

Kosher salt and freshly ground black pepper

½ cup (120 ml) heavy cream (optional)

FOR SERVING

Chopped fresh dill

Select Sauté on the Instant Pot® and heat the oil. Add the leeks and cook, stirring occasionally, until softened, about 5 minutes. Add the stock, potatoes, and 1 teaspoon salt and stir to mix. Press the Cancel button to reset the program.

Lock the lid in place and turn the valve to Sealing. Press the Pressure Cook button and set the cook time for 10 minutes at high pressure.

Let the steam release naturally, or for at least 15 minutes before turning the valve to Venting to quick-release any residual steam. Carefully remove the lid. Using an immersion blender, blend the soup until smooth. (Alternatively, working in batches if necessary, transfer the soup to a blender and blend until smooth.) Stir in the cream (if using). Taste and adjust the salt as needed.

Ladle the soup into bowls and top with dill and pepper.

Serve this rustic soup over steamed rice or with warmed naan for capturing every last bit of the flavorful broth.

Chickpea, Chard & Coconut Curry Soup

For this robust vegan soup, chickpeas and greens stud a silky, creamy broth infused with curry powder, ginger, and garlic. If you prefer a more stew-like texture, increase the cooking time by a few minutes.

SERVES 4–6

- **1 tablespoon coconut or olive oil**
- **1 yellow onion, diced**
- **2 carrots, peeled, halved lengthwise, and cut into half-moons ¼ inch (6 mm) thick**
- **3 cloves garlic, minced**
- **2-inch (5-cm) piece fresh ginger, peeled and grated (about 1 tablespoon)**
- **1 Fresno or other medium-hot red chile, diced (optional)**
- **1 cup (200 g) dried chickpeas, rinsed and picked over**
- **2 teaspoons Madras curry powder**
- **Kosher salt and freshly ground black pepper**
- **2 cans (13½ fl oz/400 ml each) coconut milk**
- **2 cups (480 ml) chicken or vegetable stock (pages 124–125 or store-bought)**
- **1 bunch Swiss chard or collard greens, stemmed and coarsely chopped or torn into large pieces**
- **1½ teaspoons sugar**
- **Fresh cilantro leaves**

Select Sauté on the Instant Pot® and heat the oil. Add the onion and carrots and cook, stirring occasionally, until they start to soften, about 3 minutes. Add the garlic, ginger, and chile (if using) and cook, stirring, until fragrant, about 1 minute. Add the chickpeas, curry powder, 1 teaspoon salt, and ⅛ teaspoon pepper and toss to combine. Press the Cancel button to reset the program.

Add the coconut milk and stock and stir to combine. Lock the lid in place and turn the valve to Sealing. Press the Pressure Cook button and set the cook time for 40 minutes at high pressure.

Let the steam release naturally, or for at least 15 minutes before turning the valve to Venting to quick-release any residual steam. Carefully remove the lid. Immediately add the chard and sugar and stir to mix. The chard will wilt in the hot liquid in about 3 minutes. Taste and adjust the seasoning if needed.

Ladle the soup in bowls and top with cilantro.

Summer Corn & Zucchini Chowder

Here, fresh corn and zucchini are paired with hearty potatoes, a creamy broth, and herbs to make the most of the summer harvest. For a vegetarian version, omit the bacon and instead cook the onion in 2 tablespoons unsalted butter.

SERVES 4

1 tablespoon olive oil

2 zucchini, thinly sliced

2 green onions, thinly sliced

1 teaspoon fresh thyme leaves

Kosher salt and freshly ground black pepper

½ lb (225 g) thick-cut sliced bacon, diced

1 yellow onion, chopped

2 cloves garlic, minced

Kernels from 6 ears corn, corncobs reserved

1 bay leaf

2 fresh thyme sprigs

2½ cups (600 ml) water

4 red potatoes, cut into ½-inch (12-mm) cubes

1 cup (240 ml) heavy cream

1 cup (240 ml) whole milk

¼ teaspoon cayenne pepper

FOR SERVING

Minced fresh chives, reserved bacon

Select Sauté on the Instant Pot® and heat the oil. Add the zucchini, green onions, and thyme and cook, stirring occasionally, until the zucchini are tender, about 5 minutes. Season with salt and pepper. Transfer to a bowl.

Add the bacon to the pot and cook, stirring occasionally, until crisp, about 5 minutes. Using a slotted spoon, transfer the bacon to a paper towel–lined plate. Grasp a paper towel with tongs and wipe out all but 1 tablespoon of fat from the pot. Add the onion to the pot and cook, stirring often, until softened, about 3 minutes. Add the garlic and cook, stirring, for 30 seconds. Cut the corncobs into thirds and add to the pot along with the bay leaf, thyme, and water. Press the Cancel button to reset the program.

Lock the lid in place and turn the valve to Sealing. Press the Pressure Cook button and set the cook time for 10 minutes at high pressure.

Turn the valve to Venting to quick-release the steam. Carefully remove the lid and discard the corncobs, bay leaf, and thyme sprigs. Press the Cancel button to reset the program.

Add the potatoes, corn kernels, and half the bacon (reserve the remainder for garnish) and season with salt and pepper. Lock the lid in place and turn the valve to Sealing. Press the Pressure Cook button and set the cook time for 4 minutes at high pressure.

Turn the valve to Venting to quick-release the steam. Carefully remove the lid. Press the Cancel button to reset the program.

Select Sauté, stir in the cream, milk, cayenne, and zucchini, and heat until hot. Season with salt and pepper. Ladle the chowder into bowls and top with chives and bacon.

Cheesy Baked Potato Soup

Kids and kids at heart will love re-creating the best bites of a baked potato with this flavor-packed soup that is served with shredded Cheddar and sour cream for finishing off each bowl. You can omit the heavy cream for a lighter consistency.

SERVES 6

1 tablespoon unsalted butter

1 yellow onion, chopped

4 or 5 cloves garlic, minced

4 cups (950 ml) chicken stock (page 124 or store-bought)

2 lb (1 kg) russet potatoes, peeled and cut into 1-inch cubes

Kosher salt and freshly ground black pepper

1 cup (225 g) sour cream

¼ cup (60 ml) heavy cream (optional)

FOR SERVING

Shredded sharp Cheddar cheese, sliced green onions, sour cream

Select Sauté on the Instant Pot® and melt the butter. Add the onion and cook, stirring occasionally, until softened and translucent, about 5 minutes. Add the garlic and cook, stirring, until fragrant, about 1 minute. Add the stock and bring to a simmer, stirring with a wooden spoon to scrape up any browned bits. Press the Cancel button to reset the program.

Add the potatoes, 1 teaspoon salt, and ½ teaspoon pepper and stir to mix. Lock the lid in place and turn the valve to Sealing. Press the Pressure Cook button and set the cook time for 25 minutes at high pressure.

Let the steam release naturally, or for at least 15 minutes before turning the valve to Venting to quick-release any residual steam. Carefully remove the lid. Use an immersion blender to blend the soup until smooth. (Alternatively, transfer the soup to a blender and blend until smooth, working in batches if necessary.) While the soup is still hot, stir or blend in the sour cream until smooth, then stir in the heavy cream, if using. Taste and adjust the seasoning if needed.

Ladle the soup into bowls and top with cheese, green onions, a dollop of sour cream, and pepper.

FOR MEAT LOVERS *Add 2–3 slices thick-cut bacon, cooked until crisp and crumbled, with the other toppings.*

BASICS

Homemade Stock

We can probably all agree that any dish made with homemade stock is better than those made with the store-bought version. While meat stocks used to require the better part of an afternoon to prepare, with the Instant Pot® you can shave hours off that time and eliminate the need to keep an eye on the stockpot. Store extra in the freezer to have on hand for quick weeknight meals.

MAKES ABOUT 3 QT (3 L)

CHICKEN STOCK

3 lb (1.5 kg) chicken parts (drumsticks, backs, necks, and wings)

2 teaspoons kosher salt

1 tablespoon olive oil

1 yellow onion, quartered

2 carrots, cut into 3-inch (7.5-cm) pieces

12 cups (3 L) water

2 cloves garlic, smashed

3 fresh flat-leaf parsley sprigs

3 fresh thyme sprigs

2 bay leaves

¼ teaspoon whole black peppercorns

Season the chicken with the salt. Select Sauté on the Instant Pot® and heat the oil. Working in batches, brown the chicken on both sides, about 3 minutes per side. Transfer to a plate as browned. Add the onion and carrots to the pot and cook, stirring occasionally, until browned, about 2 minutes. Add 1 cup (250 ml) of the water and bring to a simmer, stirring occasionally with a wooden spoon to scrape up any browned bits. Press the Cancel button to reset the program.

Return the chicken to the pot and add the garlic, parsley, thyme, bay leaves, peppercorns, and the remaining 11 cups (2.75 L) water, ensuring that the pot is no more than two-thirds full. Lock the lid in place and turn the valve to Sealing. Press the Pressure Cook button and set the cook time for 60 minutes at high pressure.

Let the steam release naturally. Carefully remove the lid. Pour the stock through a fine-mesh sieve into a large bowl. Discard the solids. If desired, pour the broth into a fat separator to remove the fat (or chill the broth in the refrigerator until the fat solidifies on top, then remove it with a spoon). Let the stock cool completely, then ladle into airtight storage containers. Refrigerate for up to 4 days or freeze for up to 3 months.

TIP *You can skip the browning step and put all of the raw ingredients into the pot instead, but keep in mind that the flavor will be milder.*

MAKES ABOUT 2½ QT (2.5 L)

VEGETABLE STOCK

Combine all the ingredients in the Instant Pot®, ensuring when you add the water that the pot is no more than two-thirds full. Lock the lid in place and turn the valve to Sealing. Press the Pressure Cook button and set the cook time for 30 minutes at high pressure.

Let the steam release naturally. Carefully remove the lid. Pour the stock through a fine-mesh sieve into a large bowl. Discard the solids. Let the stock cool completely, then ladle into airtight storage containers. Refrigerate for up to 4 days or freeze for up to 3 months.

2 yellow onions, roughly chopped

2 ribs celery, roughly chopped

2 carrots, roughly chopped

1 cup (90 g) white button or cremini mushrooms, roughly sliced

4 cloves garlic, smashed

4 fresh flat-leaf parsley sprigs

2 bay leaves

1 teaspoon whole black peppercorns

10 cups (2.5 L) water

MAKES ABOUT 2 QT (2 L)

BEEF STOCK

Combine all the ingredients in the Instant Pot®, ensuring when you add the water that the pot is no more than two-thirds full. Lock the lid in place and turn the valve to Sealing. Press the Pressure Cook button and set the cook time for 2 hours at high pressure.

Let the steam release naturally. Carefully remove the lid. Pour the stock through a fine-mesh sieve into a large bowl. Discard the solids. If desired, pour the broth into a fat separator to removed the fat (or chill the broth in the refrigerator until the fat solidifies on top, then remove it with a spoon). Let the stock cool completely, then ladle into airtight storage containers. Refrigerate for up to 4 days or freeze for up to 3 months.

VARIATION

Bone Broth: *Roast the beef marrowbones for 30–40 minutes in a preheated 450°F (230°C) oven. Add 1–2 tablespoons apple cider vinegar to the pot with the other ingredients and cook at high pressure for 3 hours. Release the steam naturally. (The bone broth has cooked long enough if the bones crumble when touched and the tendons, cartilage, and connective tissue have dissolved.) Strain and store the broth as directed above.*

3 lb (1.5 kg) beef marrowbones, cracked by a butcher

2 thick slices (about 1 lb/450 g) meaty beef shin

2 carrots, roughly chopped

2 ribs celery, roughly chopped

1 large yellow onion, roughly chopped

4 fresh flat-leaf parsley sprigs

1 bay leaf

8–10 whole black peppercorns

8 cups (2 L) water

MAKES ABOUT 2½ QT (2.5 L)

FISH STOCK

Fish stock is best made with the well-cleaned fish frames, or skeletons, as well as at least one fish head from firm white-fleshed, nonoily fish. Parts from oily, fatty fish, such as salmon, mackerel, or tuna, would give the stock a strong flavor. Rinse all fish skeletons well for the best, purest tasting, stock.

3 lb (1.5 kg) fish head(s) and frames from nonoily fish such as flounder, cod, sea bass, or snapper, cleaned

3 tablespoons kosher salt

⅓ cup (80 ml) dry white wine

1 small yellow onion, thinly sliced

1 rib celery, thinly sliced

1 fresh flat-leaf parsley sprig

1 fresh thyme sprig

1 small bay leaf

4–5 peppercorns

8 cups (2 L) water

Rinse the cleaned fish parts thoroughly under running cold water. With kitchen scissors, break the spine of each frame into at least 2 pieces. Place the head(s) and frames in a large bowl and add the salt and cool water to cover. Refrigerate for 1 hour, covered. Drain, rinse, and repeat the 1-hour soak without the salt.

Drain the fish pieces and transfer to the Instant Pot®. Add all the remaining ingredients, ensuring when you add the water that the pot is not more than two-thirds full. Lock the lid in place and turn the valve to Sealing. Press the Pressure Cook button and set the cook time for 30 minutes at high pressure.

Let the steam release naturally. Carefully remove the lid. Pour the stock through a fine-mesh sieve into a large bowl. Discard the solids. Let the stock cool completely, then ladle into airtight storage containers. Refrigerator for up to 2 days or freeze for up to 2 months.

Tomato-Fennel Broth with Mussels
(page 76)

Rice

Cooking rice can be a daunting task, not to mention a long one, when it comes to brown and wild rice varieties. This method is is quick and can be easily adjusted for your texture preference. If you like softer rice, add ¼ cup (60 ml) more water to the pot at the beginning, or let the steam release naturally for a longer period of time.

MAKES ABOUT 4 CUPS (640 G)

WHITE RICE

2 cups (400 g) long-grain white rice, such as jasmine or basmati

2 cups (475 ml) water

½ teaspoon kosher salt

Combine the rice, water, and salt in the Instant Pot®. Lock the lid in place and turn the valve to Sealing. Press the Pressure Cook button and set the cook time for 4 minutes at high pressure.

Let the steam release naturally for 10 minutes, then turn the valve to Venting to quick-release any residual steam. Carefully remove the lid and fluff the rice with a fork. If the rice feels too moist, place a dish towel over the pot and let the moisture evaporate for a few minutes longer, until your desired texture is reached.

MAKES ABOUT 4 CUPS (800 G)

BROWN RICE

2 cups (370 g) long-grain brown rice

2½ cups (600 ml) water

½ teaspoon kosher salt

Combine the rice, water, and salt in the Instant Pot®. Lock the lid in place and turn the valve to Sealing. Press the Pressure Cook button and set the cook time for 15 minutes at high pressure.

Let the steam release naturally for 10 minutes, then turn the valve to Venting to quick-release any residual steam. Carefully remove the lid and fluff the rice with a fork. If the rice feels too moist, place a dish towel over the pot and let the moisture evaporate for a few minutes longer, until your desired texture is reached.

Beans

Although canned beans are very convenient, they just don't taste the same as the home-cooked kind. Last-minute cooks, rejoice! The absolute best part about preparing beans this way is that they don't need to be soaked ahead of time. For bigger batches, double the quantities of beans, water, and oil.

MAKES ABOUT 3 CUPS (540 G)

BASIC BEANS

1 cup (200 g) dried beans, chickpeas, or lentils, rinsed and picked over

4 cups (1 L) water

1 teaspoon canola oil

1–2 teaspoons kosher salt

Combine the beans, water, oil, and salt to taste in the Instant Pot®. Lock the lid in place and turn the valve to Sealing. Press the Beans/Chili button and set the cook time for the cooking time designated in the chart below at high pressure.

Let the steam release naturally, or for at least 15 minutes, before turning the valve to Venting to quick-release any residual steam. When the steam stops, carefully remove the lid. Drain the beans in a colander set in the sink.

TIP *If you would prefer to soak your beans, soak 1 cup of beans in 4 cups (1 L) water for at least 4 hours or up to 12 hours, then cook them in their soaking water. They will cook in about half the time needed for unsoaked beans.*

COOKING TIMES FOR UNSOAKED BEANS & LENTILS

Green, Brown, or Black Lentils	15 minutes
Black Beans	20–25 minutes
Navy Beans	20–25 minutes
Pinto Beans	20–25 minutes
Cannellini Beans	35–40 minutes
Chickpeas	35–40 minutes

MAKES 12 BISCUITS

BUTTERMILK BISCUITS

In a large bowl, whisk together the flour, sugar, baking powder, baking soda, and salt until blended. Add the buttermilk and butter and combine gently with a rubber spatula or fork just until the ingredients are blended. Using an ice cream scoop, drop 12 equal-size rounds of dough onto a baking sheet lined with parchment paper. Bake in a 400°F (200°C) degree oven until the biscuits are puffed up and lightly golden brown, 15–18 minutes. Transfer to a wire rack to cool slightly before serving.

2 cups (240 g) all-purpose flour

1 teaspoon sugar

2 teaspoons baking powder

½ teaspoon baking soda

½ teaspoon kosher salt

1 cup (240 ml) buttermilk

½ cup (120 g) unsalted butter, melted and cooled

MAKES ABOUT 1 CUP (40 G)

TOASTED BREAD CRUMBS

In a small frying pan over medium heat, warm the olive oil. Add the bread crumbs, season with salt and pepper, and toast, tossing occasionally with a wooden spoon, until golden brown, 3–4 minutes. Pour into a bowl and let cool, then use immediately or store in an airtight container at room temperature for up to 2 weeks.

1 tablespoon olive oil

1 cup (40 g) fresh bread crumbs (from stale bread)

Kosher salt and freshly ground black pepper

MAKES ABOUT 2 TABLESPOONS

CAJUN SPICE RUB

In a small frying pan over medium heat, toast the fennel seeds, shaking the pan often, until fragrant, 1–2 minutes. Transfer to a spice mill and grind until coarsely ground or crush with a mortar and pestle. In a small bowl, combine the ground fennel, sea salt, black pepper, cayenne, paprika, and dried thyme and stir to mix well. Use right away, or store in an airtight container at room temperature for up to 3 months.

1 teaspoon fennel seeds

1 teaspoon sea salt

1 teaspoon freshly ground black pepper

½ teaspoon cayenne pepper

1 teaspoon paprika

1 teaspoon dried thyme

Chicken Pot Pie Soup (page 81)

INDEX

D

E

F

G

H

I

J

INSTANT POT® SOUPS

Conceived and produced by Weldon Owen International
in collaboration with Williams Sonoma, Inc.
3250 Van Ness Avenue, San Francisco, CA 94109

A WELDON OWEN PRODUCTION
1150 Brickyard Cove Road
Richmond, CA 94801
www.weldonowen.com

Copyright ©2019 Weldon Owen
and Williams Sonoma, Inc.
All rights reserved, including the right of
reproduction in whole or in part in any form.

Printed in Canada
10 9 8 7 6 5 4 3 2 1

Library of Congress
Cataloging-in-Publication data is available.

ISBN: 978-1-68188-498-1

WELDON OWEN INTERNATIONAL
President & Publisher Roger Shaw
Associate Publisher Amy Marr
Senior Editor Lisa Atwood
Art Director Marisa Kwek
Designer Lisa Berman

Managing Editor Tarji Rodriguez
Production Manager Binh Au
Imaging MJI Premedia

Photographer Erin Scott
Food Stylist Lillian Kang
Prop Stylist Claire Mack

Weldon Owen wishes to thank the following people
for their generous support in producing this book:
Sarah Putman Clegg, Carlos Esparza, Josephine Hsu,
Veronica Laramie, Nicola Parisi, Elizabeth Parson, and Sharon Silva.